Conte

Foreword

Parenting a teenager is rarely a straightforward task but for young people who have experienced early years trauma and fractured relationships the process is infinitely more complex.

How can you separate and move towards independence when you haven't experienced safe dependence? How can you safely rely on peer support when you are drawn towards peers who seem bent on self-destruction? How do you form a stable identity and set of core values when you feel fragmented and as though you have lived several conflicting lives? Sally addresses all of these issues from a parenting perspective with deep empathy.

Therapeutic parenting can have huge impacts when caring for younger children but your influence as a parent becomes more precarious as your child moves into adolescence and the process becomes (even) more complex. The empathic concern that your child might occasionally have accepted may now be rejected in a hail of insults (don't treat me like a baby, back off, stop nosing into my business) or in silence. It may seem that whichever way you approach the situation the result is the same – you feel helpless, rejected and worried and your child is isolated and trying to manage alone. In addition, the adolescent developmental process is accompanied by physical and hormonal changes, one impact of which may be that your child is bigger and stronger than you are and many creative adaptations to your parenting approach will be needed.

All of these factors make the giving and receiving of care, as well as the managing of behaviour, much more difficult for both parent and young person. Yet adolescence is a time of maturation, when your child has very high attachment needs. They may say they don't want you near them but then in the next moment are more like a toddler, wishing you could read their mind and provide them comfort. If ever there was a time when you need to 'look under' the behaviour and respond to unexpressed needs, then this is it.

Sally Donovan's book is filled with practical, real life ideas for many of the gritty challenges of parenting traumatised teens. Her good humour and ability to find something positive even in the aftermath of intense difficulties is a delight. She does not shy away from the most difficult issues and provides helpful strategies for establishing your own 'red lines' to help you decide when enough is enough, guiding you through intensely painful decisions.

What is most striking about this book is that when all ideas have failed and, as a parent, you feel utterly wrung out and despondent, there is a way to find a core and fundamental value from which you simply refuse to budge. Against all the odds, you will continue to care and show concern for your child. Sally holds firm to her belief in the value of relationships and this provides a guiding framework for her hopeful approach.

Dr Vivien Norris, Clinical Psychologist, DDP and Theraplay®
Practitioner and Trainer and Director of The Family Place

Acknowledgements

To every member of the village who has played a part in raising our family; our friends and relatives for stepping in when needed with dinners, revision, art lessons, walks and gin; the Wednesday crew and online buddies for being there with excellent peer support and friendship and those who have gone beyond the call of duty with kindness and compassion and who continued to see the best in us even when we were at our worst, the biggest and warmest thank you.

Thank you to everyone who reads and recommends my books and who generously takes the time to write reviews and share your stories with me, and to Steve and the team at Jessica Kingsley Publishers for supporting my work and for never flinching.

To my English teachers Miss Furnish and Margaret George, I don't think I ever thanked you at the time, but I've never forgotten your encouragement and your great teaching. Thank you and merci.

Lastly and most significantly, a hearty, real-life thank you to my real-life husband and children for being exactly who you are, for your remarkable humour in the face of life's sticky stuff, for your enduring love and for catching all of the small rodents.

Introduction

Way back at the beginning of the new millennium, my husband Rob and I embarked on family life with our two children, then aged one and four. Despite their early experiences of abuse, neglect, loss and abandonment they were going to be fine because they were young enough not to remember anything and we were good, capable people with more than enough love and space in our lives for these two beautiful children.

My first book *No Matter What*[1] charts the end of that fantasy and the start of our wobbly transformation into the sort of parents that our children needed us to be: therapeutic parents. It was and continues to be a difficult and complex transformation. Therapeutic parenting isn't a bolt-on to your regular, average, 'this is how I was parented' kind of child-rearing; it involves a huge change in perspective and in practice, rooted in the knowledge that early life trauma and maltreatment have a profound and long-lasting impact on our children. When the needs of babies and children are not met, when that human contract has been broken, they do not just get over it. They can't. This is about survival.

In the early years of our adoptive family life the word 'trauma' was like the big, messy elephant in the room: no one ever mentioned it. We heard about 'attachment issues' and whilst that made sense, it never quite captured the glorious whole and didn't seem to lead to many answers. As it became increasingly

---

1   *No Matter What: An Adoptive Family's Story of Hope, Love and Healing* (Jessica Kingsley Publishers, 2013).

difficult to placate us with 'well, all children do that', there was no more ignoring the big, elephant-sized thing in the room. It was stamping and shitting over everything. Nevertheless, I could dare to utter the word 'trauma' in a professional setting and might be told there was no such thing. These children were being wilfully, purposefully, decidedly BADLY BEHAVED. All of them. They just needed parenting harder, louder, stronger, stricter. But harder, louder, stronger, stricter makes things much worse, we might say, to which the reply was, 'Well, you're not trying hard enough.' I don't think so. These days I am way more confident in my experience than I was in the early days and I'll use the word 'trauma' whenever there's a need to. Trauma. Trauma. Trauma. Trauma.

My second book *The Unofficial Guide to Adoptive Parenting*[2] sets out the practical strategies that transformed the way we dealt with the baffling parenting challenges we faced. It is rooted in the comings and goings, the mess and the glory of real family life because that's where most of the good therapeutic work is carried out, by you and me, day in and day out, as we prove over and over that we 'get' our children and that we love them and stand by them no matter what. That's not to say that therapeutic parenting is a cloud of rose petals. Sure, it is about acceptance, empathy and all the rosy things but it is also about backbone, resilience and courage, tons of the stuff.

This book, *The Unofficial Guide to Therapeutic Parenting – The Teen Years*, is for all therapeutic parents, irrespective of legal or professional standing. I apply the terms 'parents', 'parenting' and 'family' in their broadest sense and I refer to 'our children' throughout in recognition that this most disadvantaged group are, in the widest sense, all of our children and we are the

---

2   *The Unofficial Guide to Adoptive Parenting: The Small Stuff, The Big Stuff and the Stuff In Between* (Jessica Kingsley Publishers, 2015).

villagers raising them. Until a couple of years ago, this was a project I didn't think I'd be able to complete. I just didn't have enough 'hard-core' experience of the adolescent years and I knew I couldn't write with any legitimacy about what I hadn't lived. I'd had bountiful experience, but just not the seat-of-your-pants type of peak adolescence experience that I knew I'd need. I got on with other things, attempted to write a novel, edited a magazine and tried to avoid emails from Jessica Kingsley Publishers headed 'The Unofficial Guide – Teens, how are you getting on?'.

Then peak adolescence arrived.

Peak adolescence and what followed wrote much of the substance of this book. I'd rather my family had been spared the peaks but I had no choice in the matter so may I welcome you to some companionship through these years that roughly equate to ages 11 to 19. I could have kicked all this off at 13, but the teenage joy ride lets you on at 11, even if you don't meet the height requirements and even if you refuse to wear a seat belt. Eleven is when many of our children go to big school, when their bodies and self-awareness are changing and when the nurture window is still (we hope) wide open.

I'm going to come right out and say it, I've (mostly) enjoyed being around teenagers. I've enjoyed the conversations, the music, the 'hey, come and look at this', the plans, the clothes, the socialising, the blossoming. A whole load of fresh experiences have come into my life that I would be poorer without. However.

Trauma plus adolescent brain is something else. Together they bring some unique and potentially extremely damaging combinations. For instance: an increased desire to search out risk and thrill-seeking, shackled to an inability to learn from consequences; the desire to move from family to peer group, with little understanding and practice of peer relationships; or a need to move towards risk, coupled with THE INTERNET.

If this book is going to be of any use to you, it absolutely has to be honest. So here goes. I have not written this to recruit potential adopters or foster carers or residential care workers, nor to discourage anyone from putting themselves forward as one of our nation's therapeutic parents, nor to get on any committee or behind any lectern, nor to be right-on and down with the kids, nor to position myself either Politically or politically. This is straight-up, no-frills honesty. When I've felt myself pulling back, as I have many times, I have forced myself to re-enter the room, put my fingers on the keyboard and write the truth as I and others around me have experienced it. The elephant is very much in the room, although a few unicorns may have suffered[3] in the writing of this book.

There has been, in the UK at least, a divide between those of us therapeutically parenting adopted children and those carrying out the same or similar parenting under other legal orders. There are of course differences between foster families, families caring for children under kinship care arrangements, adoptive families and those parenting children in residential homes and it would be wrong to overlook these differences, but there is more that unites us than divides us. At the heart of it are children who carry a burden of trauma and who can't for whatever reason live with their birth parents. They require and deserve to be raised in a way that respects their experiences and the ways they see and feel the world around them, irrespective of their legal status.

No matter what kind of parent you are, the Adolescent Trauma Years are going to be interesting. They may take you to places you never imagined you would go, psychologically and physically. The trials and tribulations you'd thought were just what other parents in support groups went through, you might go through

---

3   And no, they didn't just get over it.

too. You will see the underbelly of society and that underbelly will be mucky and dangerous and make you fantasise about moving into a gated community, or a croft in the Highlands of Scotland, or an island in Norway with an irregular ferry service. At least, that's how it's been for me. Not entirely though. We have two children and they are living these years very differently. That's mostly down to trauma and gender. Mainly trauma. Trauma is a game-changer.

If you are considering adopting or fostering a young child, or if you already parent young children, you might choose not to read on. It's a lot to take in and, personally, I wouldn't have wanted the younger years overshadowed by some of what's inside this book. What would have helped me though, was being better prepared for what lay ahead. Almost everything that has played out has been a surprise and a shock and that has made matters all the more difficult to cope with. It has meant that acceptance and other psychological adjustments have been harder to make and I've been running to catch up. This is the book I wish I'd had when our eldest child was 10 or 11. It's obviously up to you whether you read on, or not, but as a guideline, that would be my advice – dive in from round about age 10 or 11 and if you want to know the full, gory truth at any time before that, then be my guest, but you have been warned.

I should also warn you, if you didn't already know, or hadn't guessed, that there are lots of things I am not. I am not a social worker, youth worker, teacher, psychologist, psychiatrist, geneticist or solicitor. I have, however, been a frontline, extreme parent for longer than I was at school. I have listened to many great and good people on the subject of childhood trauma, attachment issues and suchlike and have stress-tested much of what I've learnt which looked like it might be somewhere close to the money. Where I haven't found the fit all that good, it could be that I wasn't trying hard enough, or that the theories and suggestions hadn't been adequately stress-tested in full battlefield conditions. I am, however, a sensible, reasonably intelligent, practical and creative person, just like you are, and I know that practice is way, way more difficult than theory. Practice takes place in our homes, within our lives, has life events thrown in the mix and THE INTERNET to contend with. It also has to happen when you share your life with actual teenagers. It is a wildly imperfect business. Several well-respected professionals have reviewed the book for possible stupidities and downright ridiculousness and if any have slipped through then that's down to me.

Since the first *Unofficial Guide* was published, many readers have messaged and approached me in person thanking me for writing the book and in particular for the permission it granted them to stop striving to be perfect. Of course we put great effort into improving the lives of our children, because they deserve no less, but there must be something in it for us too. If we are left damaged and traumatised at the end of it all then, really, what was the point? Family life isn't about putting all of your own happiness and fulfilment at the back of the miscellaneous kitchen drawer for 15 years plus. If you do that, there's a danger that when you try to find them again, there won't be much of value left. Many of us need permission to embrace imperfection and take care of ourselves without guilt niggling away. The book includes a chapter on self-care and specific ways of self-protection are woven in throughout. The emphasis is on robust and unfussy methods. I'm not big on martyrdom or meme-y bull crap.

At the end of the book you will find chapters addressed to professionals and friends and family about the considerations they might like to make when supporting or generally being around our families and children. Good, compassionate, practical support is absolutely vital through these years. Misguided support can make matters a whole lot worse. I may have been able to express a few things that you would like to say, but that, for whatever reason, you feel you cannot (my most-used emoticon is the one with the mouth zipped shut, so I know where you're coming from). If this is the case, then please feel free to photocopy the required sections and pass them on.

Wherever you find yourself during these years, whether you're on the cusp, right in the thick of it, sailing through or lying prostrate on the kitchen floor in a pool of mental agony, I wish you well and hope you find at least some unofficial crumbs of comfort in my unofficial thesis. I hope you know that in parenting, nurturing, protecting and being ambitious for your teens you are doing something amazing and life-changing and something that very few people put themselves on the line for. You may not be able to see the results right now, but all the therapeutic investments you make every day are having a huge positive effect on their lives. And no matter where they find themselves, they are equipped with the love, nurture and skills that you gave them and continue to give them, even if all that has been temporarily mislaid. Society should be a lot more thankful for what you do than it is, but it isn't quite 'getting it' yet. At the very least, our education, social care and health services should roll out the red carpet for you and your loved ones but until they really start to recognise what you do, take it from me, you're doing something amazing. THANK YOU.

Good things about sharing life with a teenager

There are many great things to celebrate about our once little children growing up and becoming teenagers. Let's take a moment to be thankful for a few of them. You're going to want to respond with a 'yes but'. The rest of the book is a 'yes but' so let's wallow in the positives for now.

No more toddler television. Television programmes and indeed entire channels aimed at toddlers are great on many levels, but too many years of it rots the adult brain. Fact.

Reducing incidents of nits. Or no nits. Imagine that. No more nits in your house ever again. No more nit combing, nit shampooing, nit checking. Literally hours of tedious toil are in the past.

Lie-ins. Not being woken up at 5am every morning has a lot to recommend it. Let's overlook the payback and the exceptions to that for now.

Bedtimes. Later, yes, but requiring hours of repetitive nightly routine, endless story time, no. That campsite you're considering staying in that is a bit noisy into the evenings? No need to worry! Been invited out to a friend's house for a summer barbeque? Stay 'til the end!

Toilet troubles. A lot less of the stinky, wet stuff to wash.

Conversations. Some of our teens are great at talking things through, expressing what's on their mind, what they're interested in, or cross about. Potentially more satisfying than 'what noise does a donkey make?' or versions of, over and over.

Films. When our loved ones are old enough to watch a 12- or a 15-rated film it opens up a whole new world of cinematic entertainment. You may even get to watch films you want to see. You may even get to watch films with, wait for it, no animated content.

Bath or shower time. Remember when bath time required copious amounts of stressful time and effort? Teen wash time no longer requires your complete involvement. Again, we're not going to go into the exceptions here.

Meals. No more nursery food.

Growing. You will no longer have to fork out for new shoes or school uniform every other month.

Risk of significant harm. Teenagers are unlikely to drown in three inches of water, run in front of a lorry, teeter at the top of a flight of concrete steps. There will be other scrapes but these will not be down to your perceived negligence. You're off the hook.

Socks and shoes. Generally, you will not have to put on or take off their socks and shoes/anorak/gloves/hat/pants ever again.

Childhood diseases. You are past the inconveniently timed chicken pox, croup, smacked cheek, weird worm-like skin infection stage accompanied by a cripplingly-long time off school.

School events. Requirements to attend events, provide cakes, barbecue sausages, dress your child in a particular colour, be unbearably nice to people you don't like, get ignored in the playground are no longer mandatory. Worth everything the teen years can throw at us, almost.

Coats. In foul weather and fair, it's their choice. No need to be *that* parent ever again. Lots of 'I told you so' opportunities.

CHAPTER 1

Adolescence

When I was a teenager, you couldn't slam a door without someone mentioning your hormones. We were led to believe we were living in a stinky chemical soup of the raging blighters and it was their fault we were drinking rough cider in parks, snogging boys with knives hidden in their socks and finding our parents unbearable. The sudden presence of hormones in our changing bodies was a cause of embarrassment and teasing. Thanks to brain imaging we now know that although hormones are playing their part, much of what we consider to be 'typical teenage behaviour' is down to the incredible changes taking place in the adolescent brain.

As I mentioned earlier, I am no neuroscientist so may I refer you to the work of Professor Sarah-Jayne Blakemore[1] for a clear explanation of what's going on inside the regular adolescent brain? Reading her work and listening to her speak has certainly helped me to make better sense of the carryings on of the teenagers in my life. It's also been interesting to map across the 'normal' adolescent behaviours and drivers with those we may commonly witness in our much younger children who have experienced early life maltreatment and trauma. I haven't

---

[1] 'The mysterious workings of the adolescent brain' (TED Talk); *Inventing Ourselves: The Secret Life of the Teenage Brain* (Doubleday, 2018).

come across any research that specifically looks at both so I'll share my observations with you. These are not just observations carried out on my own tiny data set, but include many, many families of teenaged, care-experienced children that I come into contact with. Our experiences are uncannily similar and a whole degree different from average families. Many, but not all of our young people do adolescence with bells and knobs on, they do it at full speed and at full volume and they do it with all the safety catches off.

Read any description of normal adolescence and you may be left asking 'so what's new?' Angry, rebellious, risk-taking, self-conscious, impulsive, lacking in insight and consequential thinking, disturbed sleep patterns...yeah, and? In normal adolescence the thinking, modulating, sensible parts of the brain found in the frontal and pre-frontal cortex are in partial shutdown while it works out which connections it will preserve and strengthen and which it will ditch. It's the pruning away of branches that are not required for the onward march into an independent adulthood and a strengthening of those that are. It's a process of decluttering and increasing efficiency. Many of our developmentally traumatised teens are already hampered by shoddily wired frontal and pre-frontal cortexes even before the adolescent van of workpeople turns up and the power is turned off. I've caught myself saying 'it's like his brain has fallen out' and that's certainly how it appears. Even hard-learnt skills seem to fall away and disappear. 'I thought I'd taught him that' we may wail, pointlessly. We might have, but it's checked out for now, along with loads of other skills we patiently coached them in.

Many useful life-skills are impaired during this process of brain transformation; the 'what would happen if?' ability to think through the consequence of an action, the ability to break a big task into parts and take on each one in order, time-keeping and planning, resisting the urge to do something dangerous, while resisting the urge to do very much that's constructive. The incredible pull towards risk and risky people, thrill-seeking, going to great lengths to impress others in order to fit in, the urge to fight against authority. And all this comes just when we demand so much of our young people, that they study for and sit the most important exams of their lives, that they specialise and transition out of school, that they turn away from the many risks that are accessible to them.

Most well-raised, healthily-developed teens are protected from the worst that adolescence could bring about by a number of factors. First, despite a tendency to move away from their parents, they had a solid attachment in the first place. They know in their bones they have a safe base to return to when things get a bit scary. They can do a bit of both: family and peer group, and both satisfy different needs. Second, they probably, we hope, have a peer group that looks out for each other, that doesn't run out of control and that shares an ultimate desire to do well in life. Their friends have been friends for a long time, they live in safe places, take part in activities and sports and have families that don't present a risk to them. Third, sufficient skills such as planning and predicting consequences were in place so that, despite a temporary impairment, there is still enough left to prevent disaster.

Compare that to many of our children and I think that goes some way towards explaining why they do adolescence so extremely and so dangerously. They never did quite trust our ability to parent them so they wander into danger and don't bounce back to the safety of home quite so readily. Their finely tuned fight/flight/freeze response becomes even more hair-trigger until the word 'argumentative' doesn't anywhere near cut it. They are not skilled at peer relationships but nevertheless bounce into messy peer groups, swear allegiance to people they barely know and who are far from protective. They can go to extremes in an effort to fit in and because they struggle to calculate the consequences of actions they do very risky things. Not only can they not assess risk well, some of our young people are attracted to huge doses of it. They don't learn well from even experiential consequences so, oh, here we go again with the Accident and Emergency visit or the night in the cells. Didn't they get enough of a shock the first time? No. No, they didn't. And of course they were never great respecters of authority (you can't afford to be controlled by an authority figure when you are in charge of meeting your own needs) so parents, teachers, police officers can all go f**k themselves. I may of course be way off in my amateur neuroscience and you may pick this book up in a charity shop in ten years time and laugh out loud at how ridiculous I've been. I won't care, because I'm at the age already when I don't give a s**t. That's the menopause for you, another of life's great transitions. It's come at just the right time for me.

CHAPTER 2

It's All About Us

'Kevin the teenager', the comic creation of British comedian Harry Enfield, comes into being at the moment the clock strikes midnight on his thirteenth birthday. He transforms from a happy-go-lucky, fun-filled, excitable boy into a monosyllabic, rude, obstructive, chaotic mess. This comes as a complete shock to his parents who mourn the old Kevin. Some of us have had a lot more preparation for the teenage years than Kevin's parents. Some of us barely notice the difference.

I guess what I'm getting at is that our hopes and dreams of what family life would be like were reassessed long ago and a certain amount of acceptance has already taken place. We may have learned to live with some of the sorts of behaviours that regular families think of as 'adolescence' and that we may have been living with since, like, forever. That's not to say that we don't occasionally still struggle with the realities and feel rushes of hot jealousy when we hear about what our friends and their families are up to as their children grow older and move out into the world.

When our children were small and they took up every ounce of my energy and every waking moment of my consciousness, I allowed myself to dream a little bit about what family life might look like once they were 14, 15 and beyond. This had a lot to do with how I was when I was that age: independent, out a lot, sociable, swotty. There is no doubt I'm looking back through rose-tinted specs but, you know, both my parents worked, so my sister and I came in from school, ate bucket-loads of gingernut biscuits, watched lots of television, and didn't try to kill each other or pour water in each other's beds or search the house for money or set fire to things. We had friends we went to town with, went swimming with, hung around listening to Bananarama with. We tried smoking cigarettes but that was about as daring as we got. Our independence was a relatively natural and safe affair.

I don't need to tell you that comparing our children's lives to ours at the same age is, for most of us, a very foolish thing to do. It is, however, I'm sure, natural. It's the SAT NAV we're unconsciously using as our rough guide, even though we know it's long overdue a software update. I justified my foolishness by telling myself that the enormous amount of parenting I was doing was going to have resolved almost everything attachment-y and trauma-y eight or ten years hence. I was, of course, wrong.

I think it's important to face our dreams and expectations of what we thought parenting adolescents was going to be, just like we might have had to when they were younger. Perhaps your children came into your life as fully-formed teenagers or maybe as younger children they were doing well until an enormous nuclear bomb went off, a bit like it did for Kevin, and you were left looking at the wreckage wondering what on earth took place. I know this happens. Parents will say something like 'she was amazing as a younger child, never complained, always did what she was told, was quiet, never got into any trouble, in fact the teachers at her school used to tell us that they hardly knew she was there'. Alarm bell! I have some experience of this too. I call it 'In-y Trauma' and by that I mean trauma that is kept inside, away from view and prying eyes. I know that's not very scientific.

It seems that sometimes the sheer effort of keeping this enormous thing contained and under wraps becomes too much. It must be frightening for a young person to lose control in this way. And it's a shock when parents have to suddenly face the trauma as well and learn how to support their adolescent child differently from how they are accustomed. Luckily for me, I'd had loads of on-the-job training in the 'Out-y' type of trauma, so I was more than ready (ironic voice).

Even if you've gone some way towards adjusting some of your hopes, dreams and fantasies, when the adolescent years arrive there's likely to be more work to be done.

My fantasies of these years went something like this:

- I would be in work.
- Our children would have made some good-quality friendships. These friends would occasionally come round for tea, to watch a film and chat about their stuff. They would like me, because I am quite nice and like chatting about their stuff.
- School would have become a much more stable affair, full time, with fewer if not zero meetings that I would be obliged to go to and during which would have to try terribly hard not to cry.
- College would change everything, because it's not school and you get treated like a grown-up.
- Our children would see the value of getting a good education and therefore engage with school, homework, revision and exams.
- It would be possible to leave our children home alone sometimes, like for example an hour after school, or on a Saturday morning.
- We would venture further afield on holiday and

      generally do more exciting things on the spur of the
      moment.
- Healing, development, maturity, whatever you want
  to call it would take a fairly straight-line trajectory
  meaning improvement all the way.
- Our family would not suffer some of the extremes that
  other therapeutic families around me were suffering.

Some of my expectations came to pass, some did not and others
did a bit. Things played out very differently for each of our
children. The amount of trauma they were exposed to in early
life was a massively contributing factor.

The most difficult and painful realisation was that we
weren't going to get off anything lightly. It was like every week
we ticked off something from the list of 'things that surely will
never happen', like a messed-up I-SPY book.[1] As a child I was
given the I-SPY book of *Dogs*, which is strange because I have
a phobia of dogs, but there you go, perhaps it was part of some
kind of 1970s-style exposure therapy. The rarest dogs were the
highest scorers. For example, an Irish Wolfhound would net
you 50 points. I saw one on holiday outside a chip shop and was
ecstatic, albeit at a safe distance. Oh, my goodness, there's an Irish
Wolfhound and it's enormous and I get to put a tick inside the
I-SPY box and net myself 50 whole points. I didn't feel quite the
amount of ecstasy when many years later I found myself playing
The Messed Up I-SPY Book of Teenagers and was able to tick off,
yes, ecstasy itself. And it didn't stop there. Of course it didn't. It's
a long way from spotting an Irish Wolfhound outside a chippy
in Southbourne.

As the realisation dawned that the teenage years of our

---

1   I-SPY was a set of spotters' guides for children published by News Chronicle in the 1970s.

children were going to be coloured by trauma to a great extent, I went through another wave of grief, for them and for all four of us. 'Why does everything have to be so f*****g difficult all the f*****g time?' I wailed and shouted and stomped. That's not to say there weren't and don't continue to be many great and enjoyable times because there are. But we were, and continue to be, dogged by trauma and its ways.

Who is your Default Super-Hero?

We all have super-hero costumes on under our sensible clothes and when times are tough, it's our Default Super-Heroes who run the show. It's a reaction to and a protection against prolonged stress. 'This is bloody unbearable,' says a part of our brain, 'I'm sending for Default Super-Hero.' They are parts of ourselves turned up high and out of control.

My Default Super-Hero is Captain Fixy. Captain Fixy is tenacious and gets things done, laudable traits, however, her weak points are resorting to action to avoid feeling pain, shunning self-care (it's for weaklings) and rescuing others too readily. Captain Fixy is rather a crusader, a careerist, tends towards self-righteousness and is tiring to be around. She is never so happy as when she is attempting to fix something with a system or a chart and never so unhappy as when she discovers that her endeavours haven't made any difference. Again.

A relative of Captain Fixy is Judge Drone. Judge Drone is good with detail and digging in but tends towards verbosity and can send a gathered group into a trance just by starting a sentence with 'Did I tell you about that time when?' Yes, you did, Judge Drone, and we know how long that story goes on and how long all your other stories go on for. Judge Drone is also fond of a competitive game of 'whose life is the worst' Top Trumps.

Ambassador Avoidance, on the other hand, is steady, good at

self-care and can pull off the occasional stunning performance under difficult conditions; however, he withdraws under a heavy duvet with a remote control for prolonged periods during times of stress and 'checks out' of life. He will go to almost any lengths to avoid a confrontation and if things were left to him no one would ever go on holiday, eat a meal, or receive a birthday present. Captain Fixy and Ambassador Avoidance are each other's nemesis.

I'm being flippant, of course, but there is something more serious behind the flippancy. When we are living with and parenting in the face of trauma it is incredibly taxing and we can lose sight of balance, reasonableness and the art of the possible, sometimes at great expense to ourselves and our partners and to the detriment of our children. We get called back to Default Super-Hero headquarters and take our orders from there. We behave in rather extreme ways and get on people's nerves. We become stuck and rigid and can make the same mistakes over and over again.

So much of therapeutic parenting is learning when and how to over-ride our unconscious and automatic reactions and responses. For this reason we need to know which Default Super-Hero outfit we reach for when stress levels are high and we must from time to time force ourselves to put them back in the wardrobe. Therapeutic parenting is a lot about self-discovery. When you start out, they don't tell you that these children are going to teach you so much about you.

Red Buttons

Red Buttons: we all have them, buttons that when pressed send us shooting up into our emotional stratosphere. WHOOSH! Off we go whilst some of those around us watch and wonder what on earth just happened. Others may be pleased that aiming for your Red Button had exactly the desired effect.

The whole business of Red Buttons is illogical. My Red

Buttons will be different from yours. You may look at mine and find them ridiculous. 'What do you mean the smell of Lynx Africa sets you off?' In my defence, it's not a waft of Lynx Africa but clouds of it, so thick in the air you can taste it. Some Red Buttons are woven into who we are, like being set off when plans are delayed, and others develop out of experience. When they have a strong association with unpleasant and memorable events perhaps some are more like triggers: enormous sensory Red Buttons.

Just as Red Buttons are personal to us and our experiences, our reactions to having them pressed can be different too. Some of us (me) may show great tolerance for quite a long time before then going off like a box of fireworks. Others may have a more 'slow-release' reaction. I can usually soak up a firing of a single Red Button, but keep pressing it, or press a few in quick succession and I go bananas.

Many people leading ordinary family lives can go along for most, if not all, of their years, never experiencing what it is like to live with a full range of Red Buttons. That's not the case for most therapeutic parents. We get to discover ours in intimate detail. Lucky us.

The reason that our Red Buttons become so prevalent and powerful is, I think, because many of our children need to identify them and press them in order to find out what we're made of, to control the emotional temperature of the house or as a proxy for their own WHOOSH (it perhaps feels safer for someone else to enact it on their behalf). Some children will also press the Red Buttons belonging to their siblings. Poke. Poke. Poke. It's a good way of getting your brother or sister into trouble and keeping attention away from yourself. One thing is for sure, in our house anyway, some children are expert at locating other people's Red Buttons. I was tempted to write 'and exploiting' there, right after 'locating' but that would make it sound more intentional than I think it is.

Most of my Red Buttons are so illogical they shouldn't even be Red Buttons, but they are. In the face of them I find it almost impossible to muster a therapeutic response, or even to take helpful and well-intentioned advice. In fact, helpful and well-intentioned advice just makes things worse.

Here are some of my Red Buttons:

- The sight of an item of stationery, belonging to me, that has been used shabbily/destroyed.
- The use of the word 'mate' as applied to someone of very recent and perhaps virtual acquaintance.
- Being referred to in private or in public by the term 'mate', particularly when the 't' is dropped, or 'yo blood' (even worse).
- Homophobic, racist, sexist, disablist views delivered with rampant superiority and with no due reference to facts.
- Pro-Trump propaganda, particularly justified by 'and my mate's dad agrees with me'.
- Gang and penitentiary chic.
- Waste.
- Being late.
- The smell of Lynx Africa.

I am not proud of any of the above, far from it. They reveal much about my snobberies, age and weaknesses and how easily I can be hijacked by things clearly designed to set me off. Often I can see the racist remarks, or whatever, for what they are: an attempt to press my button, and I can shrug them off or respond cleanly, or if it were, let's say, my birthday and I was to be driving home after a not completely enjoyable meal in a pub I might blow a casket and on the return have to remove myself to the bottom of the garden to spend several hours feeling murderous and then depressed before I can calm myself down enough to come inside the house. Not that that's ever happened, you understand.

I have found two ways of dealing with my Red Buttons. First, I've had to be entirely honest with myself about what my Red Buttons are. Second, I've shared with my family what most of them are and the likely result if any of them were to be pressed along with a casual interest in why it might be that certain people seem a little bit keen to find them. The flaw in my approach is of course that it means handing over the nuclear codes to someone whose frontal lobe isn't working as well as it could be (and I hope we're not all about to discover where that takes the world) but it does mean that a preventative therapeutic intervention may be made, for example:

'If you continue to talk about the Paralympics in this way, I'm going to have to walk out or I might lose my temper.'

'Look, I should have removed myself rather than shouting, but it set me off when you flashed that massive gold watch in my face and called me "mate".'

It may also create the opportunity for a conversation involving the whole family about all of our Red Buttons, but that's the Advance Therapeutic Course in Red Buttons.

For those of us parenting as a twosome I believe it can be helpful to talk about each other's Red Buttons in as accepting a way as possible. You know you're heading in the same direction when you can while away an entertaining hour in the local garden centre cafe talking about how you reacted when you discovered your only good lipstick had been trodden into the carpet and left for dead, or how you wanted to punch yourself in the face during a protracted and heightened conversation about vaping that you know shouldn't have set you off, but it did.

The point of being able to pinpoint and laugh at our Red Buttons is because they are at the same time both pathetic and powerful and laughing helps us deal with the shame and the pain of difficult things.

Acceptance and hope

In the first *Unofficial Guide* I wrote about the process I'd had to go through in order to accept our family life as it was and cut loose the fantasies that were haunting us, fantasies such as the vibrant family meals we were going to share during which we would debate the issues of the day. Your fantasies will be different from mine and maybe you've found it easier to let go of yours than I did mine.

To really and completely accept a child, particularly one whose difficulties aren't, shall we say, expressed in entirely socially acceptable ways, is much more difficult than it is made out to be. I thought I'd done all the acceptance that there was to be done, together with the letting go and the grieving and the raging, but as adolescence arrived and blossomed I realised I had a whole lot more accepting to face up to. There are times when I've had to accept that the only way I can hope to get through with my mental health intact is to pretty much have no expectations at all, to take what comes and roll with the punches. That's not to say that I gave up, not at all. I learned to keep hope carefully protected. Measured and realistic hope is incredibly powerful. It's hope that gets me to meetings, prepared and focused. It's hope that navigates me through the confusion of services. It's hope that keeps me building relationships with each new professional that comes into our lives. It's hope that has driven me to continue putting one foot in front of the other. Sometimes I've had to have enough hope to go around. And before you start to think I'm some kind of angel of hope, in the interests of honesty I must admit that there have been times when I thought hope had been extinguished. It hadn't, but it did go on a few extended vacations (unlike us).

The reality was that the gap between our family and the 'normal' families around us grew wider and wider until I would come home and cry after spending time in someone else's house, in and around their normal family bustle. My expectations were completely wrong in lots of respects and coming to terms with our reality was, and sometimes still is, very difficult.

During our darkest times, reality has meant police, drugs, thugs, stealing and estrangement and it's meant f**k you and all you stand for. When I thought things couldn't get any worse, they did. It's easier now I understand that some of our children have to try it all and hit rock bottom, that they will graduate from vapes, to fags, to cannabis and right the way down to Class As without passing Go. I know how it works and I know how much I can influence these trajectories, which is not at all. Accepting that has honed my therapeutic skills and my self-care. Reality can be a bastard but it's better to know he is than to be taken by surprise.

Your reality may be nowhere near mine, and I hope for your sake it isn't. But I wouldn't mind betting that whatever your situation, you face some meaty life acceptance challenges. It's worth remembering that we all approach acceptance differently; what I might struggle to accept, you might find a breeze and vice versa. It comes down to our own histories and to those pesky stakes in the ground: values. Again I've been forced to examine each of my values and again, some of them have turned out not to be values but hopes and dreams in fancy dress and some of them, well, I'm still not sure what they were, vanity perhaps.

My family history is emblazoned with stories of escape from gruelling poverty by virtue of hard work, grit, determination and night classes. These stories are powerful, not only because they have taught me about hope and hard work, but because they have instilled a deep fear in me of not having any money. Mr D is from similar stock and our attitudes towards money, saving and work are closely aligned and deeply engrained. We could no more change our attitudes than change the colour of our eyes. We live well but we buy second-hand, our tech is a few generations behind, we shop around, we have savings in case the boiler breaks down or my Ford Fiesta needs new brake pads. Well done us.

And yet.

Young people burdened by trauma cannot always 'try' themselves better, plan a way out, work their passage to a better life. Our familial and societal hero stories about working-class graft are a poor fit for a young person who hates going to school, who would rather do almost anything than revise for an exam and whose frontal lobe isn't working and they certainly don't fit a young person who believes in their bones that they are rubbish and always will be. Why bother trying when you're that bad? The hero stories were a bad fit for Mr D and me too. As well as burdening our family, such hero stories made self-care feel like outrageous laziness. I guess I still hold by hard work, saving and frugality as a way of living a good life but I accept that these make no sense to a young person who can't see a good future, let alone plan for one, and whose brain has fallen out.

If you've made it as far as adolescence then I'm certain you'll already have had to undergo a certain amount of pruning of rules and values. Yours, like ours, may have undergone quite a radical pruning. I'll be frank – as adolescence blossomed, the vast majority of our remaining rules went out of the window for reasons of being either unachievable or only achievable at the expense of our sanity and safety. When I refer to rules and values, you'll understand that I don't mean hanging up wet towels, putting rubbish in the bin, bringing mugs down from bedrooms. These are small fry, 'nice to haves'. In our house there are almost always bigger things to worry about. Don't get me wrong, we're not savages. When the time is right, when things are calm, I might ask for the 12 cups and their mouldering contents to be brought down to the kitchen. But if someone has just returned home after a difficult day at school, then I won't.

I think our kind of parenting means we have to get down to brass tacks. What are your absolutes? What are you going to die in a ditch over? Where does reasonable allowance end and encroaching on the rights of other members of the household begin? These are important and difficult questions that most families do not have to wrestle with. You may not have to either. We have and some of our conclusions have left us rather gasping for air.

When adolescence plus childhood trauma brings about times of complete crisis, rules and values will need radical reappraisal, but that's not to say that some of those rules and values shouldn't remain in place, even if they move into the background for a while. A time of crisis is a time for special measures. If we get through a period of crisis, then perhaps an amount of normal service should resume. There's a sliding scale of rules and values in our house, depending on where and how everyone is. What has been crucial is the establishment of stakes in the ground, those hard boundaries that don't move. In our house these are not hurting anyone else, not bringing drugs into the house, not taking what belongs to someone else and not staying up all night and keeping everyone else awake. Clearly these will be different in your house. I think we became a pretty extreme case.

As our children grow up, more of their mistakes will be made in the outside world: at school, college, in the workplace, in the street. We have stuck to our philosophy of not double-punishing something that has been punished elsewhere and that lasted us well. It didn't stop us advising and encouraging thinking skills around risk-taking and consequential thinking and expressing our horror when we really were horrified. We must still be there to catch our children when they fall, to help them through the inevitable feelings of shame, because the fundamentals of therapeutic parenting still apply. We will, however, have to step back more often than we step forward and give our children the space to resolve their own problems rather than rush to the rescue. It's an ever-changing dynamic, though, and one of the factors is the extent to which we must emotionally protect ourselves. Being clear about which is our emotional load and which is our child's is very important. At the risk of stretching this analogy too far, as they grow up, we can't carry their load, but we can help them to be strong enough to carry it for themselves.

The tanks of empathy

Much of the first *Unofficial Guide* was about seeing the world through our child's eyes, connecting to them and their early lives with empathy and using this to give our parenting meaning and relevance to them. During adolescence that's as relevant and crucial as ever; it may also become much, much more difficult. In my experience, empathy has its limits.

It's relatively easy to empathise with a cute child, with their wide eyes and tiny hands and delicious way of talking, even if that child has had an early life that clouds some of the cuteness. We may spot them from afar, say in the playground, catch them engaged in an activity or glance at them sleeping and our empathy tanks are topped up. You don't need me to tell you that adolescents, especially our older adolescents, may be a little less easy to connect with on this level. We can find our empathy tanks running dry. And what's more, we can find ourselves being the last bastion of empathy, as everyone else loses the stomach. It really can be a shitty wicket.

Here's how I've tried to keep my empathy tanks topped up:

- Learning about the changes that take place in the adolescent brain and remembering that for our traumatised young people, those changes take place with knobs on. They wrestle with life's big questions when their brains are in a state of semi-shutdown, plus they have a fragile sense of self. It's a massive ask. No wonder so many of our young people experience huge struggles at this time.
- Occasionally returning to their file and reminding myself of their early experiences. These great big smelly adolescents are still those small, vulnerable children, but in a bigger box. I have a set of photographs that act as a shortcut. During our most difficult times I glance at them and that's enough. There was a time when I wished I'd never laid eyes on those pictures. Now I'm glad I have them because they explain so much. 'Look,' I can say, 'it's TRAUMA.'
- Looking after myself. Living in a permanent or even semi-permanent state of secondary trauma and stress makes empathy difficult and inauthentic. In order to top up empathy I believe it is essential to have time

away from the person we are working to maintain empathy with. That might just be me. I need some space and separation and time to reconnect, sunlight, fresh air and simple carbohydrates. Self-care is the biggest act of empathy we can make.

· Allowing in my prejudices and Red Buttons. There are some aspects of modern adolescence that I can't bloody stand, especially the extreme versions. This is probably evolution's way of telling me that it is time to separate and to let go. What evolution doesn't take account of is the developmental delay caused by early trauma that makes the pull of separation come well before our children are developmentally ready for it. I think it's OK to dislike gang-cool, pimp-style, young offender-chic as long as I suppress it in front of my nearest and dearest. I don't suppress it in private, because I am not a robot and it's got to come out somewhere.

· Going to the occasional training day and conference. I need to keep hearing the messages again and again. Each training I go to I learn something new and something rings true that hadn't previously. Training days help me to regain some objectivity and a sense of community. We really are in this together, even if we feel alone, and it's good to connect with our fellow travellers and return home refreshed and able to continue.

Despite its obvious benefits and all-round goodness, empathy is not always what it's made out to be. It's kind of become all the rage and a by-word for feeling someone else's pain so intensely it means you are saintly and righteous and people are miraculously improved by your presence. It's very public, very 'social media' and teamed with a 'tilted to one side' head position and a slightly unhinged sing-song tone of voice; it really is something to crow about. But that's pretendy empathy, not empathy (and it brings me out in acts of imagined violence).

For us, empathy is not being casually acquainted with a suffering person and taking them out for an occasional latte, but living with that person 24/7, through thick and thin, and shit and stinky shit. Empathy, the real deal, is a much tougher call altogether and requires a whole other level of strength and courage. As Dr Brené Brown explains,[2] empathy is about taking the perspective of another, like climbing into a dark cave with a person, not merely peering down at them from above and shouting down nonsense. I like that analogy. However.

If one stays down in that cave perspective-taking for too long it can become more a feat of self-flagellatory endurance than an act of humanity. We may start to forget there is any kind of life outside the cave, we develop rickets, poor eye-sight and trench foot. We might even start to own the perspective, like it's ours. One day we may wake up on that cave floor, after a damp and disturbed night's sleep and realise we are both trapped down there, weighed down by misery (and the rope ladder is rotting away).

The cave has to be for short trips only and not gap years or longer stays. There are times when a trip down Empathy Caves is not even possible and not even helpful. Sometimes chucking down a head torch and a Bounty and saying, 'It's sunny up here, why not come and join me when you're ready?' (in a non-sing-song voice) is the best we can do. Pretendy empathisers may misinterpret this as cold-hearted and mean. What pretendy empathisers don't get

---

2   'The power of empathy' (YouTube video).

is that you are an empathy Olympian employing smart thinking and advanced methods, not an empathy fun runner.

One of the potential pitfalls of therapeutic parenting is that empathy becomes some kind of cure-all. If we could only muster up enough empathy we can win at trauma. If we're losing ground then it's because we're just not being empathic enough. Empathy is not self-sacrifice. Empathy isn't giving your teenager a stick and asking them to beat you with it, and it definitely isn't commiserating with them when they can't hit you hard enough.

Grief

Grief might seem like a strange word to use in relation to therapeutic parenting. Selfish perhaps. A bit hysterical. Grief is the only word I know to describe a specific mix of waxing and waning feelings around the gap between how we imagined our family life was going to be and how it really is. The gap isn't just that created by our imagination and our fantasies, it's a gap we see everywhere we look, a gap created by trauma and society's blindspot to its destructive forces.

At its worst, this kind of grief doesn't result from a one-off event like the death of a loved one, it can feel like death by a thousand cuts. Some of our children make the most incredible progress, others struggle at every step, maybe because their burden is heavier and their trauma deeper. For the latter group we observe the gap between them and their peers grow from a hairline crack to a chasm as opportunities whizz by at the wrong pace and at the wrong time. Many of those opportunities are one-time-only offers, our children time-out and are washed up in an adult world with few of the skills and capabilities required but all of the responsibilities.

If we sat in this massive grief for too long, the sadness, anger, injustice and guilt would drive us mad. And yet, if we ignore grief for too long it has a way of building up behind the wall of the dam and eventually breaking through at its weakest point. I know I'm not alone in sometimes feeling like I might get drowned in it.

As well as grieving for my loved ones, I also grieved, and sometimes still do, for myself. Some may ask what I've got to feel sad about and I wouldn't expect anyone who hasn't lived this life to understand. I don't always understand it myself. It doesn't come from the best part of myself, so to be honest, I'm a bit ashamed of it too.

The grief I feel is complicated and contradictory. I feel great sadness that our family life has been so constrained and ruled by trauma and yet that constraint is what our children needed in order to experience some recovery. I feel sad and angry that repeated mistakes and aggressive and controlling behaviours have brought such terrible unhappiness and distress into our home and yet I know about the ultimate causes: massive dsyregulation as a result of massive trauma. I almost need it to be someone's fault, but it kind of isn't. I've wanted to blame the child, blame the adults who should have kept them safe, blame the services who kept telling us it would all turn out all right, but, ultimately, not even blame helps. Action helps a bit and that's why much of my onward energy is focused there. It doesn't stop me wanting to yell, at the top of my voice 'I TOLD YOU SO!' In this instance though, there is no victory in being right. Not many of those who ever said to me 'all children do that' are still on the scene, so I couldn't push the contrary proof in their face, even if I wanted to.

Trauma has laid waste to weeks and months and years of our family life. We had and have many happy and fulfilling times and I am certain that we made the best of what we had and what we knew. I'm not into regret, so although there are a few things

I'd have done differently if I'd known then what I know now, I'm proud of us all. But there is something for me on my own to grieve: the life I thought I would have as a parent and a woman with ambitions and hopes and dreams. We may hear 'well, you did choose to do this' and yes, we did. But was it really supposed to be like this?

I guess what I'm trying to say here is I think it's all right to feel the grief and all its perplexity and its nonsense. Let it wax and wane, wax and wane and get on and create a new life, with the imperfections and the wisdoms woven into it. As always, a big part of this is self-care, self-care and more self-care.

CHAPTER 3

Chaos

The one word I would use to describe the peak adolescent years in our house is 'chaos' and it's chaos I have found to be my biggest personal challenge and chaos that has exposed the weakest of my weak spots: a need for order, systems and a degree of dependability and predicability. That's Captain Fixy for you.

Having said that, I don't think I'm particularly extreme in that department. I'm reasonably untidy, a bit lazy and I've never been into doing the laundry or the shopping on the same day every week but I had not appreciated the degree to which my own ability to organise my life was rooted in my stable upbringing until I became a parent of traumatised adolescents. I guess we all have our own preferences and needs when it comes to how we order our lives.

I have friends whose children's trauma presents itself as the very opposite of chaotic, needing to keep tight control, so I know that this trauma business can work in very different ways. This chapter, however, is going to focus on varying types of chaos and the ways we might understand, accept and work with it.

Drama Llama

Most of us get a kick out of hearing about a bit of a drama from time to time: somebody left their husband and ran off with his best man, a neighbour has recovered from a life-threatening illness. Kind of all right to talk about these distant dramas for a bit and then move back into normal life. Not so all right to actively seek out mega-dramas, to feed off them and get off on them. A man was taking heroin in the multi-storey car park, someone was slashing themselves with knives, a homeless person was being attacked. We may have to hear all sorts of horrendous things with some frequency. We may be peeling carrots at the time, or reading a book about trees.[1] It may come at us like the most jarring change of tempo. Even if we've heard it before, we may not be expecting it in that moment at all. Violence, murder, bleeding, attack, danger, drugs. It's not too difficult to work out where some of this might originate from.

I had some good advice about how to respond to Drama Llama:

Exercise curiosity. Ask about the event, how it came about, where it took place, how it felt to witness it.

Match the energy. Use a similar volume and tone of voice: 'Wow, that must have been a shock!'

Deploy empathy. Wonder how it must have felt to witness the incident, wonder how it must be for the victim, are they all right, what happened to them?

I. Could. Not. Do. It.

I tried, but most of the time I just could not respond therapeutically with any authenticity. When I did OK, very little I said was right and I made things worse. I sympathised with the wrong person, I misunderstood, I under-reacted or over-reacted.

---

1   Thomas Pakenham, *Meetings with Remarkable Trees* (Phoenix, 1996).

The roots of Drama Llama are, I suspect, complicated. A healthily raised teenager's brain will drive them to seek-out thrills, but generally not really dangerous, seedy threats. No, the seeking-out threat thing is, I reckon, about having lived in a dangerous environment, it's about threat detection and moving towards threat as a way of keeping safe, it's about feeling alive and it's our old friend dysregulation. Dysregulation and a brain wired for thrill-seeking are a match made in hell. Both can potentially drive our adolescents into frightening situations where their vulnerabilities are exposed. Of course they won't like us to warn them that they are making themselves vulnerable because we are adults and parents; teenagers reject the influence of their parents and traumatised teenagers may never have trusted their parents or any other adults anyway, so double, triple, quadruple whammy.

For me it's been useful to know what's behind Drama Llama although it hasn't necessarily helped in the moment when Drama Llama has burst through the door agitated, excited, wide-eyed, big, loud, intimidating and aroused. Better to say to oneself, 'watch out, it's fight/flight/freeze' than 'I'll reach for the Gun of Logic and Reason'. The Gun of Logic and Reason is on first sight an impressive weapon against the forces of fight/flight/freeze but has a barrel that bends back on itself and is aimed at the shooter. I've shot myself in the face with it many times.

Often the best policy in the moment was to offer food and get out of the way, avoid any kind of reasoning, avoid logic, avoid opinions and warnings. I also got good at planning where I was in the house when I anticipated it was coming: standing up, doing something active like cooking or the washing-up and not a passive activity like reading or working at my desk.

As with other manifestations of dysregulation, the real weapon was working out what was causing the dysregulation and tackling that. It might be a bus journey, going to a particular friend's house or an exam. We get good at trigger control, but as our children grow older, it becomes more and more impossible to avoid the triggers, especially as trigger avoidance may be experienced by our children as parental over-control.

> *'I've noticed that every time you take the bus you come home triggered up.'*
>
> *'I'm going to pick you up from school this week and we'll see if that improves things.'*
>
> *'I'm happy for you to have your friend here, but I don't want you going to his house again soon. It was too difficult for you last time.'*

Ideally, we have the opportunity to explore the triggers with our children and they allow us to reduce the triggers for them. But this is real life and real life doesn't work like that. The conversations should still be had though, because these are the conversations that demonstrate critical and consequential thinking, love and compassion. I think it's OK to say things like 'I can't stop you going there, but I need you to know it worries me when you do because you come home in a bad way' with our older ones and 'you're not going to like this, but we're going to have a weekend of family time to get everyone grounded and calm' with our younger ones.

I'm a fan of Close Supervision and although it becomes more and more difficult to carry out with older children, I hung on to it as long as I could and used elements of it way into adolescence. Close Supervision is used with young children when things are spiralling out of control and you find yourself wondering which of the current top ten mega-problems you're going to prioritise. You know those times: Meltdown Central along with disappearing food, a self-inflicted haircut, wet beds, toys down the toilet... The theory is you put in dawn-til-dusk nurture and togetherness that creates calm and safety and reduces opportunities to 'fail'. Done consistently over a good long time, it rewrites the dysregulation and 'failure' patterns and starts to create belonging, success, happiness and enjoyment. It can only be done when we are in the right mind-set and when we pour in a ton of self-care.

Depending on our children and their ages, Close Supervision can still be carried out with our older ones, albeit probably in shorter stretches and more stealthily. We have to be creative in our approach and sometimes come from left field. Days out to favourite places, the outdoors, the seaside can all be holidays from the dysregulatory realities of life.

As well as trying to work all this stuff out for my children I've also examined my own standpoint when it comes to Drama Llama and beware because this isn't going to sound terribly accepting. Constant verbal (and sometimes real) exposure to the seedy side of life, the bullies, criminals, drug users, thugs, is toxic. I can't bear it. I don't want to bear it. Exposure to it reduces my ability to be therapeutic, full stop, and it weighs me down and pollutes my psychological environment.

I'm at the point now where I am hyper-sensitive to violent dramas. I cannot watch violent films or TV programmes or Jeremy Kyle-esque confrontational shoutathons. Recently I was watching a reality show about a group of civilians who undertake the Special Forces selection course. It involves carrying out almost impossible physical tasks whilst an instructor shouts things like 'What the f**k do you think you're f*****g doing!!' in their faces. As the volume of the shouting increased, my heart rate rose and my tiny and exhausted adrenal glands started pumping out stress hormones. I had to switch off, make myself a milky drink and read a book about trees.

If you want to better understand the waves of drama that blow across your family life I recommend the work of writer and rapper Darren McGarvey.[2] Darren grew up in a deprived part of Glasgow. In an interview,[3] he said, 'I adapted to the fact my mother was not fit to look after me... From my mother's behaviour what I learnt was that I lived in a dangerous and hostile world full of people that couldn't be trusted.'

And in another interview,[4] he describes travelling to the West End of Glasgow, the affluent side where he notices the calm and the quiet. People aren't shouting and in each other's faces, offloading their anger and walking around in a constant state of fight or flight. During times of stress, some of our young people cannot cope with living in our calm and ordered homes and it's such a discord and a discomfort, they are driven to turn up the volume and import some of their inner drama. When that hits me, when I'm peeling carrots or reading a book about trees it's like we are coming from different sides of the city, different cultures.

Darren McGarvey talks passionately about his own recovery that has come about through acceptance of the circumstances he found himself in and taking responsibility and claiming agency. I've learnt a lot from Darren's work and it's helped me to realise that there has to come a point when we pass over the agency and the baton to our young people. That's not to say we stop caring, or we stop advocating for opportunities, but we cannot up emotional sticks and metaphorically move across the cultural divide. We wouldn't survive.

2   Darren McGarvey *Poverty Safari: Understanding the Anger of Britain's Underclass* (Luath Press, 2017).

3   'I saw the hate in mum's eyes', The Daily Record, 2 November 2017

4   BBC Radio 4 – Start the Week, Anger and deprivation, 13 November 2017

Tech

Not only is tech expensive, highly desirable, addictive and triggering, it's ridiculously fragile. Yes, tech is the gift that keeps on giving.

I could write an entire book about trauma, starring the mobile phone and co-starring its bigger brothers, the tablet and the games console. Between them they have more to show us when it comes to trauma than any other objects I know, and that's even before we get to the internet, which I'll cover in a later, more excruciating chapter.

First, the reasons.

A dysregulated, state of fight is pretty risky for any smartphone or tablet nearby. Something's going to get thrown and that something is likely to be something to hand, something loaded with meaning and something that can deliver rejection in an instant. What can follow is terrible shame and self-loathing, which only makes the likelihood of further smashing even higher.

Being in a rush most of the time, because trauma fills your head and makes you move fast to avoid sitting in the horrible discomfort of the moment, is also very dangerous for smartphones. Being put right on the very edge of a table, being carried precariously with two other objects in the same hand, being carried in the pocket of a sweatshirt as the wearer swings out of a car are all dangerous situations for smartphones. One small 'dink' is all it takes.

If the smartphone user hasn't yet perfected their fine motor skills then normal handling can be a dangerous business for smartphones too. Likewise if the user is sensory-seeking then buttons and covers are removed and replaced and removed and perhaps bitten and...you've got the idea. This is the real-world collision of biological and developmental age.

Control is another factor (isn't it always?). If a child's default is that adults are not to be trusted, then an adult bearing a protective cover and a screen protector is definitely not going to be given the time of day.

Consequential thinking is what drives most of us to use protection (and I may or may not be referring to more than smartphones). How likely is it that my phone will at some point get dropped? Very. What would happen if I dropped my phone and had failed to use protection? The screen would most likely smash. How would that make me feel? Really p***ed off with myself. Difficulties with consequential thinking mean that the questions don't always get asked and if they are the answers would be something along the lines of 'ahhhh, it'll be fine'. When it's not fine, when the screen is cracked, or worse, it will of course be your fault, 'cos shame.

Here are some ideas for mitigating against broken tech and its consequences.

Massive amounts of acceptance. These things are going to get broken and the more you come to terms with that the easier it will be, for everyone.

Massive amounts of not caring. I don't mean not caring in an uncaring way, I mean not caring in a not being emotionally bought-in way. My way of anaesthetising myself from the pain of another five hundred quid being dropped in the bath is not to spend five hundred quid in the first place. I have become the queen of second-hand tech. There's loads of it about and if you use the right sellers it's reliable and guaranteed. I also wouldn't go near a contract which can so easily turn into shelling out 30 quid a month for some piece of broken crap that doesn't work anymore. Let me tell you, that would trigger me and my inherited 'make do and mend' mentality sky high.

Massive amounts of live what you preach. This is a personal one so may not work for you. Because, as I mentioned earlier, I worry about running out of money and becoming starving and homeless, I would never ever spend a large amount of money on a phone. 'Yes, so and so may have a brand new fourth generation whateveritis and they're only 12 but I don't care, that's not how we do things in our family. The lovingly-sourced, not quite as up-to-date, second generation whateveritis will have to do, and look, that's what I've got too, in fact mine is not as good as yours.' You may have had similar conversations in your house. They won't work with the doggedly determined and they will highlight that baffling overlap between trauma and a raging sense of entitlement that I struggle with to this day. Sometimes we have to quietly stick to our values and wait for these things to play out.

Batten down the hatches. When a major, destructive storm is brewing and it is safe to do so, remove the tech, I repeat, remove the tech.

A ready supply of lecture-free protective cases, covers and screen protectors. For younger children, consider a 'no protector, no phone' rule.

A massive supply of empathy available for when the phone gets broken. 'You must be so disappointed', 'you must have felt terrible when you picked it up and saw it was cracked?', etc.

A savings scheme for the purchase or part-purchase of replacement tech. We all care more about things when we've worked and saved up for them, don't we? I don't know, but in my quest to link work with reward, investment and ownership I think it's worth a try. Again, this is a long-term measure.

In most parenting books, this is where I'd counter with something about how wonderful these devices with their lovely fragile screens are and their access to so much knowledge and opportunity, but this isn't most parenting books so I'll spare you.

The Black Hole of Desire

It isn't difficult to understand why some of our children may struggle to feel satiated when it comes to food, but what about objects?

Adolescence is commonly observed to be a time when the desire for material items increases and brands and styles are used as a way of self-expression and self-identification. Expensive trainers, jeans, sports shirts, make-up, watches and smartphones become a way of fitting in and of communicating belonging with a particular tribe. Tribes are important during adolescence as young people move away from family and seek belonging in a surrogate 'family' to ease their way into independence.

How much more complicated is it for our children? There is evidence[5] to show that materialism in adolescents peaks at the same time as self-esteem dips. I feel rubbish about myself therefore I will buy things to make myself feel better. It's not a concept that's alien to even the best adjusted. Acquiring scratches an itch, but perhaps only momentarily and if that itch is a black hole that swallows things up, how will any amount of acquiring ever satisfy?

Many therapeutic parents notice not only a rampant desire for material objects in their children, but also a difficulty in valuing and caring for objects once they have been acquired. I wrote about

5   Christian Jarrett, 'The psychology of stuff and things', *The Psychologist*, August 2013.

the tide of broken objects that swept across our house in the first *Unofficial Guide*. Adolescence has put a slightly different, and of course more complex, spin on things.

I'm going to struggle to express this part without coming over as judge-y, but in the interests of honesty here we go... There is something more going on around the acquisition of huge amounts of tat: tat that breaks easily. The postman has delivered rivers of tat into our house. The more the better. Quantity over quality. Trying to scratch the unscratchable itch. If materialism is linked to self-esteem then there is no better metaphor. Belongings as an extension of an under-valued, fragile, fractured self and the act of purchasing as a way of keeping moving, avoiding the terrible pain of stillness and what might rush in to fill the space should stillness persist.

The criticisms that we may hear ourselves levelling at our teens and their materialism, before we've engaged our therapeutic better selves, perhaps give away something deeper about self and about shame.

'You buy all this rubbish.'

'You don't value your belongings.'

'Why would you want to dress like a criminal?'

Certain looks and brands become identified with a sort of criminal underworld and these can be the brands some of our young people are drawn to. Sometimes it's brands that might appear bizarre to us, like North Face. Out there on the streets the objective of wearing a North Face coat isn't to keep the wind and the rain off, it's to send a signal that you are well hard. The more powerless you feel inside, the stronger the tribal messages you have to send out, the bigger the brands, the more flashy the watch, the jazzier the trainers. The artist Grayson Perry nailed this in his Channel 4 documentary 'What Makes a Real Man'.[6]

I've taken time to understand the reasons why and as ever I've learned that this search for self has to be played around with, experimented with and, of course, it is likely to be explored in opposition to us as parents. I daren't even express that I don't like a brand because as sure as eggs is eggs, it will be waved in my face before I can shout 'polyester sportswear'. We have to disapprove, and that's the point. But. (There's always a 'but'.) Trauma drives the materialism to darker places. Rivers of broken stuff, risky stuff, stuff that advertises vulnerability, stuff that screams 'I'm a piece of s**t'.

When our young people leave home and their belongings are packed up in a bag, that's when it may hit us, that this child that we and our extended family and friends have showered with lovely things over years of birthdays and other celebrations, has very little left, of material value, that hasn't been broken, lost or sold. It's incredibly sad and it may challenge our own deeply held values. At the centre of it, however, is a young person with a fragile and fractured (broken) sense of self and we may have to hold on to hope and think of the nice things we will give them in the future.

I can't give you any clean, easy-to-follow advice, because for me this is psychologically very complicated territory. Thinking about all the stuff, lovingly chosen, bought and wrapped, that we invest something of ourselves in, that is then trodden on, broken or sold is painful. I've tried to adopt a more vaguely spiritual approach, but I'm no Buddhist monk: to give without expectation and in giving to let go of the gift in an emotional sense. I've sometimes scooped something up and put it away

---

6   This was the second episode in a three-part documentary series called *All Man*. The clip I refer to is available on YouTube: 'Young Gang Members on What Makes a Real Man' (Channel 4).

when I know it is at risk now but will be desired in the future. And I've hung on to the definite truth, that the best we give of ourselves is our time, our compassion and our constancy over years and years, because that's the gift that our children need more than they may realise.

Bedrooms

Tides of empty wrappers, plates, mugs of decomposition, bits of biscuit, dirty pants, the remnants of the clean laundry pile you once put on the end of the bed, a DVD without a case, a tissue containing some revoltingness, other unmentionables, wet towels that smell of dead animals, an unpacked bag from a long-forgotten weekend away, vapes, fags, lighters? I feel your pain, believe me.

There appear to be two schools of thought when it comes to our teens and their bedrooms. One is that we should leave them to live how they want to, not interfere, not get triggered by the mess into shouting about the place and winding everyone up. The other is that because they are not developmentally ready to take care of their own space we must intervene in order to prevent complete chaos breaking out. I must confess to flip-flopping between the two and although the better part of me favours the intervention, the knackered part of me generally leaves the bedroom well alone.

Once in a while I will carry out a deep clean. This will take so much longer than I had expected and while I'm filling carrier bags, wondering if I oughtn't to be wearing rubber gloves, I'll think of that scene in Blade Runner and like a mad woman will say out loud 'I've seen things you people wouldn't believe'. Afterwards I will impress on my child the importance of keeping the bedroom how I have left it and allow myself to feel slight optimism. This will be dashed. I will shout and wind everyone up.

I suspect that this is the best I will ever be when it comes to the question of bedrooms.

I will, however, share with you a really useful piece of advice given to me by my friend Jenny.[7] She told me that no matter what, and even and especially when things are unutterably terrible, I should regularly wash the bedding in lovely-smelling laundry liquid so that comfort and nurture can be delivered silently and through smell. Smell is very important and so too is demonstrating that you are thinking of your child, even when they can barely function in the family home at all. Jenny is always right about these things.

Late

I make no bones about it – I hate being late. Hate it. Can't bear it. Being late really makes me lose my s***.

I factor float time into my arrangements and then some more float time just in case. I'll be found on a deserted railway platform a good 25 minutes before the train is due to arrive, even though I only live five minutes from the station. You see, there may have been a slow-moving tractor on the road, an unexpected diversion or a flash flood that extended my journey time. If I get held up and my float time drains away I have to hold down a rising tide of panic by talking to myself or, in extremis, singing. If it's something really important, I'll leave hours before I need to or take the train before the one I need to, just to be sure. Whenever my alarm goes off before dawn I am reminded I am a little bit unhinged when it comes to being on time. When the second, reserve alarm goes off even the cat raises her eyebrows.

---

7   Jenny, writing as Hope Daniels, author of *Hackney Child* and *Tainted Love* (Simon and Schuster, 2014).

There couldn't be a greater contrast between my sense of urgency around time and that which plays out in my household. It has been one of my greatest challenges and I have had to work hard to understand time and the challenges it presents from the point of view of my nearest and dearest. I have also had to work hard to dampen down my 'we're going to be late!' screeching mega-trigger.

When our children are small, we can take charge of time for them and act as the proxy time management bits of their brain. We may also be able to exert a certain amount of control to corral the unwilling and to safeguard commitments. As adolescence dawns even the insufficient amount of control we had seeps away. Ensuring someone catches the bus, gets the lift, turns up for work on time can become a torture and, for me, did become a torture.

We measure and root ourselves in time through repeating patterns and structures: minutes, hours, days, light, dark, weeks, months, seasons, birthdays, celebrations, and each of these breaks up time and helps us make sense and navigate our way through it. If young children struggle to learn to tell the time and to recite the months and how many days make up a month, for example, then I guess it's no wonder that as they grow up, they struggle with the intricacies of planning and time management. Feeling awash in time must be disorientating and confusing. I think this is what's going on and I reckon that if we could gaze into the traumatised, adolescent brain, the bit that's meant to be in charge of time management would be laid back on a beanbag with its pyjamas on, taking a nap.

What got me thinking about this in terms of brain development was this: I would say something like 'It's 10.30 and we need to be at Toby's house by 11.30, so we need to start getting ready now.' The response would more often than not be 'But we've got a whole hour.'

Toby's house is half an hour from our house, I would explain, to looks of complete bafflement. In their minds, we would be teleported to Toby's house in no time. The school bus would arrive at 8 o'clock, which would equate to bag packing and shoe putting on at 8 o'clock. I cannot tell you how many times I have explained the concept of preparation and travel time. It doesn't stick, because I think the requisite part of the brain is not functioning sufficiently well. And then there's the control double-whammy – I'm not listening to your advice because trusting you feels unsafe. It may sound hysterical, but I have come to think of it as brain damage.

If it is brain damage, then given the ability of the brain, even the traumatised brain, to learn new skills, the remedy is practice and repetition. For as long as our young people allow us to, we need to put the structure in place for them and demonstrate the structure and point out the patterns that play out day after day and praise when some of this starts to stick. The difficult patch comes when developmental age possibly requires a visual timetable or suchlike and the biological age says 'f**k off, I'm not a baby.' So when our children are towering over us, certain that we are wrong about absolutely everything, especially the time the bus leaves, how do we go about family life without driving ourselves nuts?

You probably shouldn't take any lessons from me, but in case you are a time slave too, here are the approaches I took:

- As much not caring and not being emotionally bound up in another person's demonstrable lateness or catastrophic time management as I could muster.

Shrugging. Gritted teeth. The dynamic in many of our adolescent-rich homes is that the more we demonstrate we care about something, the more likely it is to be trampled on. I've aimed not to become ensnared in this dynamic.

- In times of calm, explaining the plan for the following day.
- Printing off bus timetables and suchlike and displaying them in prominent places.
- Prompting with as little emotion as possible, 'have you checked the time?' or 'you need to be thinking about using the bathroom.'
- Making the wifi available only when the 'getting ready' has been done.
- Letting lateness play out when it didn't impact on other members of the family. Being as sympathetic as possible when the lateness has wrecked a plan. Accepting that the real learning comes from repeated and sometimes excruciating experience.
- Allowing flexibility where possible, for example I might arrange a pick-up after a trip into town at a particular time, and accept 15 minutes either way. The same for an agreed 'be home by' time.
- A close to zero-tolerance approach to missing the school bus. I learned from experience that missing the school bus really messed things up for all of us and gave the responsibility and the burden of the consequence of being late to the adults in the house. If you're 14 and you can be on time when it suits you, then you need to learn to be on time for school. It's important to remember whose shoulder the monkey should be

sat on. Let's face it, there are enough monkeys crowded onto our shoulders without adding more.
· Secretly adding in half an hour float time to arrangements where possible. This can take the pressure off and prevent the mega-trigger from being pulled.
· Teaching how to use a smartphone calendar and reminding to put appointments in, with alarms.

We may eventually have to witness our young people stepping out into the world, with a shaky independence, missing appointments, being late for work, and losing jobs and friendships as a consequence. We will also watch them learning the skills they need and using some of those skills we fought to teach them. One day they may even acknowledge that the knowledge and skills you passed on have been of great benefit to them and you'll able to smile to yourself and imagine the little bit of brain development that you had your hand in encouraging.

Money

Budgeting, saving and wise spending are essential life-skills and essentially about life. The mature, well-formed brain is generally pretty good at working out necessary outgoings related to shelter, warmth and nourishment and, whether we know it or not, most of us are inadvertently using Maslow's hierarchy of needs[8] when we do it. We move up through essentials like shelter and warmth, to items that keep us and our environment clean and safe, to transportation and to expenditure on things that make our lives better like entertainment, furnishings and things we like to wear.

8   A model developed by American psychologist Abraham Maslow in 1943.

If we're lucky, most of us know about this stuff when we leave home and if we don't we learn pretty quickly. We may already have saved up for things like car insurance, or a new phone or a holiday. We've learnt to live with the disappointment of not having enough money to do everything we want or to buy everything we desire. We've accepted that sometimes maths gives the answer as 'no, you can't afford that' and that the consequence of buying something means we can't buy something else. Either or. Difficult choices.

Overlay the skills required to manage money with the skills our children struggle with and there lies the trouble. How often do we say to ourselves that our child has little consequential thinking, struggles to plan, cannot picture a better future, just can't hear 'no'. To add more into the mix they may be dysregulated by having money and spend it quickly and randomly, they may have transitory 'friends' who only appear when our child has money in their pocket and may be driven to use money to acquire food. Attitudes to food and money are I think heavily symbolic of trauma and survival. Money may get burnt through in a haze of trauma-fuelled fog and what follows is the resulting hangover of shame and self-loathing. Good people spend their money wisely. Good people save. I am bad, I am bad, I am bad.

The answers, as far as there are any, are about us, their loving parents acting as the thinking and planning parts of their brain, for as long as they will allow us to do so. By doing this we not only save them from 'failure' and shame but we model good practice, over and over and over.

As I've mentioned before, Mr D and I are rather tediously infected with the whole 'rewards for hard work' thing, which has proved to be rather, let's say, challenging for us both in the face of not only rampant spending but also a strong and weird sense of entitlement. I'm not sure there are two more ill-fitting sets of values and behaviours you could put together. As our family grew up and it became more than a possibility that flying the nest wasn't going to be a straightforward matter, we realised that we were going to have to teach a link between work and reward. I know, how old-fashioned of us. We gave an amount of No Matter What pocket money that was paid in cash and then latterly into a building society account and another amount that was in payment for a small, easy and quick task. Making that link has, I think, paid off, although at times it was a massive headache. ('I'm not doing my job, eff off, not doing it.'/'That's fine but you know that means you won't get the money.'/ 'F∗∗k you, I want the money.'/ 'You can have it if you do the job.'/ 'But I'm not doing the effing job, you're a t∗∗t...' Yeah, you know the drill.)

As if all this weren't complicated enough, the equation might include the additional factors of Stealing and Siblings. If you don't have either of these extra layers to wrestle with, then skip this paragraph, or risk feeling the desire to throw yourself into a lake. If a member of the family is a little light-fingered, then it is of course pretty much impossible to leave any money around. If you have siblings who are light-fingered with each other's money, then, well, you don't need me to paint that particular picture for you. We managed for quite a while with lockable money boxes before we graduated to building society accounts. We graduated way too early.

When you open a bank or building society account for your child, you have a meeting with a bank person, who assumes that everyone's brains are functioning well. They will ask you questions like 'would you like a card that allows spending online and in shops, or just one that can be used in a cashpoint machine?' Because you are sensible and have already thought through the consequences of a dysregulated child in possession of a bank card that works online and in shops you will reply 'cashpoint only please' while your child looks daggers at you. The bank person will look at you as though you are a monster. There are no winners here.

Some of our children will be pleased with the 'cashpoint only' card and will manage it perfectly well. Others may take the restrictions as a giant 'NO' and do everything they possibly can to convert their card into a 'buy any shit I want from the internet' version. If they succeed (what am I saying 'if'?) then you are probably in for a teeth-grindingly difficult time when it comes to money and what money can buy. You will waylay the postman, open packages not addressed to you, marvel at the contents and perhaps throw said contents into the wheelie bin. You may discover that despite it being illegal in many of our fine democracies to lend money to under-18s, there are loopholes the size of a shipping container that your child will find and exploit. You will end up paying the debt, and it may be impossible to do this therapeutically. Someone who has been a great help to our family calls it Sledge Hammer Learning. It's when the same mistakes with the same horrible consequences are made over and over again. When the brain scientists talk about learning being like walking repeatedly across a field of wheat, treading down the plants and wearing a path until it is there forever, well, those wheat plants sure have a tendency to persist in popping back up.

While the path is being trodden, our children may indulge in spending their money in ways that are really very inadvisable indeed. I'll talk about that in the chapter 'Risk-Taking', but for now, just think of bags full of sweets, only worse.

Here's some good news! Some families find those cards that can be loaded with money via an app work for them. The money can be transferred in small amounts, quickly and when required. We've had some success with a Virtual Savings Account. This is the notes section of my phone where I record each week how much has been earned for carrying out an agreed job. The money can be exchanged for something material, of real value. We use it as a way to save up for big things. When the savings are cashed in for, let's say, a phone or a pair of trainers, then the idea is that that item is valued more because it is representative of work carried out. It's not perfect, but it kind of works for us.

When our children become young adults and the dreaded Credit Consumer Act gives them access to vast amounts of borrowing and on top of that perhaps benefits or wages are paid in lumps, we have little ability to influence anything and I'm afraid it is pretty much down to Learning the Hard Way. While our loved ones are Learning the Hard Way we will again have cause to reflect upon how deep trauma may run and the hidden disability that again puts our young people at a great disadvantage compared to their peers. You may find yourself having to decide how far you will consider rescuing them from the financial trouble they get into, whether a rescue attempt will give them enough breathing space to work things out for the better or whether repeated rescuing is just delaying the inevitable Learning the Hard Way. Either way, it can be incredibly difficult and there are perhaps no right answers and no neat solutions. Generally we try to help out by providing food and other essentials rather than money or items that could be exchanged for money and we have so far avoided paying off debts owed to 'friends' although I can't honestly say we would never do this. As I alluded to before, risky behaviours can lead our loved ones into very dangerous territory indeed.

Personal care

Sensory issues, triggers, organisational problems, spiky profiles, identity, shame, control, dissociation: hygiene and self-care is about all these and more.

Unfortunately, biological age marches on, without a second thought for whether children are ready for the additional self-care burdens brought about by puberty or the adolescent brain. One minute they are happily playing in the bath and allowing us to wash their hair and huggle them out into a fluffy towel, the next they are resisting running water, ignoring our pleas for them to get a shower or clean their teeth and slathering on make-up and hair gel as though these will somehow achieve the same effect as soap and toothpaste.

How we wish we could hold back time for a bit longer, allow more time for the basic lessons to stick, but we can't, just like we can't hold back school transitions or exams or the age of majority. Growing up gets all out of kilter, like it does for many teenagers, but as you know, ours do it with bells on and that's because they have a lot more to contend with than the averagely soap-averse teen and because personal care and hygiene is about the body, a body that may have been subjected to abuse and neglect.

Those with sensory issues may not like the feel of shampoo or soap, they might find the cascade of water droplets in a shower too much to take, or the squeak of clean skin unpleasant or the pull of a hairbrush painful. And sadly some of our children are disconnected from their bodies and don't know how they smell or feel, how greasy their hair is, how smelly their socks are. And they are going to find it difficult to be helped and reminded, due to the enormous levels of shame that can come with being perceived by others as being dirty. We may find ourselves wondering how we hadn't noticed some of this before and that might be because it wasn't that obvious before. And it might be that some elements of trauma are not drawn out into the daylight until the circumstances are right. Remember when your children came to live with you and everyone but everyone told you that they were potty trained and dry through the night and within a few weeks of moving in with you, they were regularly wetting during the day and needed a nappy at night? And how that took years to improve? Well, it goes to show that this parenting business isn't about linear progression. It's more like a computer game where extra challenges get unlocked along the way. Personal care and hygiene is a big extra challenge and it's waiting patiently for its stinky time in the spotlight.

I can remember the hatred I felt for my body when puberty happened and I had nothing other the usual body-shock going on. I try to put myself into the shoes of a young person who has suffered body trauma and understand why they become disconnected and ashamed and wouldn't want to undress and wash themselves.

But no matter how empathic we think we are, who can honestly say they aren't triggered into disgust by a close-up of a set of yellow teeth and a gust of hot, stinky breath? Who doesn't recoil at a nostril full of ripe body odour or stale urine? This is basic and instinctual and that's why it's so problematic. If we find it difficult to over-ride our reactions, it's because it is. It's quite possibly impossible. We have to find ways around our hard wiring to continue to nurture our great big children.

For most of us, with our functioning sensory systems and our regular amounts of shame and our desire to be accepted by the tribe, being noticed by another person for being dirty and smelly would be about as mortifying as it gets. Our brains don't take well to social exclusion; in fact they experience it as true pain. I think if are brutally honest with ourselves, our brains also seek to distance us from those we perceive to be dirty. Perhaps it's a primitive drive to avoid disease and stay alive. When we venture out into the social world with our slightly less than fragrant but nevertheless loved teens, our brains just don't know what to make of it all. Reject child? NO. Feel disgust? YES. Show disgust? NO. Worry about others showing disgust? YES. Worry about child being rejected? YES. Experience frustration that child can't just take a shower? YES. Feel narked that their hygiene somehow reflects on our own hygiene? BIG YES. It's a matted and filthy confusion. How do we turn down our responses and get on with the business of therapeutic parenting?

It would be a relatively easy job, if it weren't for the other b*****d factor in this and that's our old friend, control. Some of our nearest and dearest have an almighty need for it and no less so when it comes to matters of the body. No matter how annoying and frustrating control is, it's about survival, so there's no shooing it away with a hairbrush and a wet flannel. This is, I'm sorry to say, another task for the slow, steady, empathic approach, if necessary with the windows open.

Here are some of the approaches that I have found helpful, or that my friends have, or that I wish I'd been able to employ but didn't have the energy for:

- Provide a ready supply of shampoo, soap, shower gel and other unctions. If your house is like mine, then buy cheap and pile high and remember that quantity used may not directly equate to cleanliness. Where does it all go? Who knows but try not to think of it as pouring your money down the drain.
- Think 'developmental age' (way easier than it sounds).
- Model good personal care: 'I've had a busy day, I really need a shower'-type of thing.
- Accept that you will have to be the laundry fairy for a very great many years. Gather up, sniff, sort, wash, rinse and repeat.
- Accept that natural consequences are inevitably going

to have to do some of the heavy lifting. You go to school smelling unpleasant, it's a matter of time before some kid notices and says something in front of all the other kids. Be there to pick up the pieces when this has happened. 'That must have hurt', 'Here I've bought you a bath set', that kind of thing.

- Put a cheap roll-on or spray in the bathroom, bedroom and in the school bag and the PE bag. The day that kid says something, you might be the hero that saved the day.

- Accept that you will see and smell things that no parent should ever have to see and smell. It's part of the deal. It's difficult to keep this stuff to yourself, so share with someone understanding. We all have a story. Mine involves a shoe box and that's as far as I'm willing to go with that story.

- If you can, indulge the make-up, hairstyle, fashion interest by watching YouTube videos and buying 'products' together. I still can't apply a perfect eye-flick but I can do a mean fishtail plait. This also counts as big time sensory nurturing.

- Sometimes we really have to insist that the shower is taken. 'I don't often insist, but today I do.' You know the kind of days: weddings, a trip to a crowded cinema, a family birthday party. The best of us put attachment above everything, but in my world, there are some things you can't turn up to smelling like a tramp.

- 'You smell good' and 'your hair looks cool today' are the sorts of things we can drop in at unexpected times. Not best deployed straight after the forced shower and not in large, obnoxious amounts. Like all kinds of praise, small and quick in and out is best.

Control

Chaos sometimes comes in a neat, tight wrapping of control.

I'm fine. I'm fine. I'm OK. I'm ready. I've done it. Shut up. Stop nagging. I'm fine. I'm fine.

But the body language, the flicking eye movements, the fidgety feet, the chewing of the fingernails, the sleepless nights, the food stash, the self-harm give the game away. Some of our children learn that the very last thing you do is to admit you're in difficulty. Others may sing and dance away our concerns, in a 'nothing to see here' act of diversion. The metaphor of the swan is a good one: serene and in control on the surface, paddling like billy-o under the water. As therapeutic parents we have to get good at looking beneath the surface, not listening to the spin-doctor.

There are myriad different ways that our older children can get into difficulty without us knowing anything about it: bullying, troubles with friends, getting behind with homework, stressing about a test, making a mistake on social media. They may stick their head in the sand and hope it will all go away, while meanwhile it grows bigger and bigger and more and more overwhelming. The need for control dictates that asking for help is extremely difficult and experienced as vulnerability. I've got used to being Detective Inspector Mother. I can tell when something isn't right and I've had to get good at gentle delving and I've had to prove over and over that when I know the truth I'm not going to react by busting a blood vessel. When I don't bust a blood vessel I am invariably met with great surprise, because I am not behaving in the way their early experiences tell them adults behave when they are displeased. 'I am not that abusive adult' I have to prove, over and over and over. Sometimes I think that's my main job in all this.

When I suspect there's some great big bubbling boil of chaos that's about to burst, my 'go to' approach is this:

- Prepare myself mentally for the conversation I need to have, think through my strategy, process some of the anger and frustration I probably feel to avoid reactionary statements such as 'you posted a picture of your what?' or 'I asked you if you had any homework and you told me you didn't!'
- Some of the ways in might be statements like: 'because I care about you I've noticed that something seems wrong and I want you to know it's OK to tell me, I'm not going to be angry'. I may have to follow this with a jokey 'look how laid back I am today, nothing's bothering me'.
- Other ways in might be some surprise nurture, sweets, a nice pudding, a trip somewhere in the car (to try to bring about car-sharing)[9], something that says 'I've noticed you're struggling and I'm here' without actually saying it.
- Be prepared for the long haul.
- Be ready to hear something which might be a giant Red Button and have the 'thanks for telling me, now we can work it out' response at my fingertips.
- Once the sharing has taken place, show myself to be capable and trustworthy. I may have to insist I share with another adult in order to resolve the situation, for example a hideous build-up of homework may have to be shared with school, likewise bullying.
- Check in regularly: 'I'm dealing with it', 'how are you doing?', 'here's a hot chocolate, I thought you might need it'.
- Be prepared for the boil to burst messily anyway.

---

9   Deep conversational sharing taking place during a car journey, usually on a busy road lacking in lay-bys.

I might go so far as to say that modelling this kind of acceptance and dependability is what really fuels change and the development of trust. And when our loved ones grow older and potentially get into more serious scrapes, if they have some trust in us, this might make all the difference.

CBA

If you've never sent your child a text asking them to do something for you and been met with the response CBA, then I'll enlighten you: CBA stands for Can't Be A∗∗∗d.

Would you mind putting out the bin?
CBA.

Would you bring down your laundry?
CBA.

Please collect up the dirty cups.
CBA.

Get your homework done.
CBA.

We're leaving the house in half an hour. It's time to get up.
CBA.

Newton's First Law of Motion explains this phenomenon pretty well: an object at rest stays at rest unless a force acts upon it causing its speed or direction to change. The greater the mass, the more force will be required to change its speed or direction. Unfortunately the only force that can act on our large masses and get them moving is us and we're already burdened with our own inertia. That's not all Newton had to say about parenting.

His Second Law of Thermodynamic Parenting states that basically everything turns to s**t: the tidy drawer, the pristine school pencil case bursting with new contents, the clean toilet bowl. It's a lot more complicated than that, but it does explain CBA and what happens when CBA gets its way.

CBA is the homework not getting done, the school uniform having to go a second week, being horribly late for an important appointment. It looks like laziness and that's part of the story but not all of it.

CBA is a head too full of keeping afloat to think about much else, it's avoiding facing something that is associated with shame and failure and it's another sign of difficulty in planning and imagining the future. Why would you get out of bed on a Sunday to do your homework when you know it's going to be rubbish and you can't think about the consequences of not doing it? It's also a lot about control, of course it is. At its most extreme it's perceived as a lack of ambition.

I tell you what it also is: it's really annoying. I get tired of being the force regularly exerting itself against the power of inertia and I get tired of clearing up the resulting chaos. 'All teenagers, blah blah blah...' I know, I know, and yet... I witness nothing that even registers on the same scale in other families. In fact, when I spend time in other families I come away exclaiming 'and that's why I'm so tired!'

This is what I try to do to combat the inertia and get some bloody velocity going:

Who loses out if the thing doesn't get done? If it isn't you then seriously consider the natural consequence. 'This is the last time I'm advising you to get out of bed and do your homework,' then walk away and do something for yourself. Being late to meet a group of friends in town: again, is that you who suffers? Needing to get out of the house as a family is a different matter. Build in float time and consider a wifi interruption.

Getting on with life. Our beloveds can benefit from observing that the family gets on with having fun whether or not they join in. Is it really healthy for one member of the family to regularly prevent the others from doing things aka having a life? Think about creating a life that your beloved wants to be part of. This has been one of the game-changers in our family.

Getting enough sleep. Some of our family members may be extremely sleep resistant. I'll go into the whole sleep thing in another section, but for now, it's worth considering whether CBA is 'I was on my phone all night' or 'I was watching repeats of Love Island'.

Reflecting back. At the end of a successful day, when inertia didn't win out, reflect on what a great or successful time was had. Repeated reflecting back like this may help to develop cause and effect thinking ('I managed to be arsed and actually enjoyed myself').

Protecting ourselves from chaos

If you share your life with a chaos generator then you will know the toll it can take on those of us with a rather lower chaos threshold. When chaos is bearing down on me it feels like a game of Tetris on the most difficult level: the faster I place the shapes, the quicker they rain down upon me until my brain shouts 'enough' and all bets are off. Living in chaos for prolonged amounts of time does, I believe, leave us open to catching a bit of chaos ourselves. Here are some of the ways I've tried to protect myself:

Stripping back life. Where I can I've made changes to make our family life as simple as possible. This has involved cutting back on stress-inducing activities, saying 'no' more often and making small, micro changes like cooking simple, quick meals and stockpiling kit like stationery and school uniform.

Decluttering the house. This has been a gradual enterprise, when and if I have the headspace and when there is sufficient space in the bin. I've found that the sparser my home, the more capacity I have to cope.

Accepting a level of chaos. Easy to say and I've had to work at this one.

Deciding where you can tolerate chaos and where you can't. I can't do chaos in our living room or in the bathroom, so that's where I focus my attentions.

Pick a few small rules and work on them. I decided that when conditions allowed I would train (for want of a better word) willing and unwilling participants to undo one little piece of chaos. It might be bringing a wet towel down from a bedroom, or clearing up the plates after a meal or sorting out the recycling. Quick and easy tasks have worked best. Take care not to get into mission creep ('bring down your towel, and all the cups and put your clothes away') because I think we know where that ends up.

Grant yourself a break from worrying about chaos. I sometimes do a 'what's going to happen if I don't worry about this' analysis. Often the answer is that the situation remains unchanged, but I am freer from worry. Much of this stuff we can't influence that easily anyway and worrying never helped anyone.

Be wary of 'fixy' fixes. Those of us who love a bit of action and fixing may have to resist the temptation to fix our children out of the chaos. Little bits of 'fixy' might help, but in the long term it's feelings of safety and belonging that really ace this, not charts and systems.

Here's some good news, kind of. As our children get older, other adults in their lives, such as teachers, expect them to be able to take an amount of responsibility for themselves. Problematic though this is, we may find ourselves blamed and pestered less as it becomes more apparent that we are not the generators of the chaos.

CHAPTER 4

The Internet

The internet. Never has anything in the field of human endeavour unintentionally caused so much stress to so many therapeutic parents. It's almost as though it's been designed to exploit each and every one of the vulnerabilities of our young people, it does it so well.

Don't get me wrong, I am a fan of most of the internet. I use it to listen to podcasts about science, watch documentaries about art history and identify unusual birds that land on my bird table. What I don't do is use it to send pictures of my genitals to unsuspecting colleagues or arrange to meet complete strangers in railways stations. I also don't tend to throw large items of furniture when my access to the internet is restricted.

For many of our young people the internet is one giant challenge and we'd better be ready for it, despite the services around us and the tech giants being almost wholly unready or unwilling to back us up.

The most common criticism levelled at parents seems to be 'why can't you just ban them?' or 'you just need to put in the right controls'. My response to that is 'well, if it's that easy, don't you think we'd be doing it?!'

We, my friends, are in the unenviable position of being at the forefront of possibly the biggest change in human social interaction ever. If that weren't a challenge enough, we who grew up pre-internet are raising relationally damaged young people who struggle with social interaction in the real world, let alone in the virtual. When even 'normal' families are battling to keep their well-functioning young people safe, how do we stand a chance?

Now and again, the internet will throw up an article about how to encourage safe internet usage in children. Most of the advice causes me to dysregulate because most of the advice is written by those whose experience is limited to raising well-regulated, well-attached, probably high-performing children who aren't yet ten years old. Suggestions like 'write up a contract and make their signature a condition of them accessing the internet' and 'insist they friend you and make you part of their internet friendship circles' are hilarious. I want to ask the authors of this tripe what planet they are living on. Not Planet Hyper-Risky that's for sure.

In this chapter, I'm not going to pull any punches. If your child functions well on the internet, listens to advice and will accept certain controls, then skip over it. If, however, they struggle to hear the word 'no' and would rather do almost anything than take any single piece of advice from you then read on for the full horror and for some hard-learnt tips from me and from some of my friends.

Here are some tips for starters:

Keep your child away from the internet and from social media in particular for as long as is humanly possible. Children who have gaps in their social and emotional learning need maximum experience through real-world relationships. They need attachment and regulation and they need us. Our children also need adults to adult-up and not give them access to technology that is likely to bring about 'failure' and the resulting feelings of shame.

Educate yourself. You need to know about the social media platforms young people use and about controls and risks. Use social media yourself, get to know how it works, get to know the unspoken 'rules'. It's a different world from the real world, it evolves quickly and, in order to keep our children safe, we need to be part of it. It doesn't mean we have to immerse ourselves but we do need to have a good working knowledge.

Decide on the rules right from the start. It's no good walking in blind and then deciding you might need some rules, you'll just end up stamping all over their human rights. Rules I like are:

- Tech to be kept somewhere other than the bedroom at night-time.
- The internet will go off at bedtime.
- The internet will come on once you are ready for school.
- When necessary we will have a tech break.

I think fewer, cleaner rules are better. Accept that constant attempts will be made to break the rules and they will cause much pleading and agitation. You will of course be the only mean parent enforcing such draconian measures, blah, blah. Stick to your guns. There are always households around with no rules, but it's the children in these households who fall asleep in lessons. Sorry, not in our house.

Our teens are not alone in having adverse reactions to being without their tech or wifi. Where they can differ is in the scale of their reactions. In some of our households the threat of removal of a phone or the wifi going off at the end of the day can be a 'run for cover' moment. And yet access to tech and wifi can in itself bring on levels of dysregulation that rock the entire family.

Can't live with it. Can't live without it. The jury appears to be out on whether games, apps and social media are addictive, but as their design is based around trying to soak up as much of our time as possible and employs psychological principles in order to do so, I think we can say that our children are at least as likely to become welded to their tech as their peers are. I'm no brain scientist, but I'd bet that their traumatised starts in life leave their brains more open to the compulsive pushes and nudges than those whose childhoods were built on more solid foundations. And their difficulties in negotiating their way in the real social world are magnified in the virtual. Yet again, their vulnerabilities make negotiating the modern world so much harder.

Some years ago, when we were going through rather a tricky time, I spent six months playing Candy Crush. I did other things, but not many of the things I should have been doing. Meals were late and had missing components and I would get to bed in the early hours after a long session and have a rabid sleep plagued by boiled sweets and vats of caramel. I knew I was using Candy Crush to escape mentally from 'life' and yet I felt compelled to move up through the levels without any idea what the ultimate aim was. It did not make me happy, in fact it made me the opposite. Eventually I realised I was being controlled by algorithms and kicked the habit in favour of reading, reconnecting with friends and setting light to things.[1] Although I've never gone back to Candy Crush, or anything similar, I can waste hours scrolling through social media and come away feeling worse. What are we doing to ourselves? And what are we doing to our children?

Some clever people liken the age of the internet to the invention of the printing press and use that analogy to argue that social media and the internet is just another invention that we oldies are going to have to get used to and stop panicking about. The one significant difference between the printed book

---

1   Specifically, lighting huge bonfires.

and the internet is the product. We exchange money for a physical book and that's the contract we enter into. What's the contract when we use 'free' social media and what exactly is the product being supplied? In his book *Move Fast and Break Things*,[2] Jonathan Taplin argues, 'If you don't pay for it, you are the product.' The product is our attention and it's our attention that is being sold to advertisers. Our attention is being harvested and sold on for profit. It's all rather alarming when you look at it this way. But it does go some way towards explaining why our teen calls us an effing whatever and throws their phone at us the moment the wifi goes off. They were busy having their attention harvested and quite enjoying the experience. We, their parents, have no chance against this kind of psychological skulduggery. This has been my rather long-winded way of reassuring you that the dice are well and truly loaded against you and your zero-profit parenting. If you feel as though you're swimming against a very strong current, then that's because you are.

As I've already set out in the previous section, setting the boundaries right from the start is, I think, key to future success. Without these boundaries, no young person would ever get a good night's sleep and our lives would be hellish. We had other boundaries like no tech at the dinner table that gradually slid as children got older and tech at dinner became the least of our worries. Something we have always done is to give prior warning that a meal is going to be ready, or we need to leave the house: a happening that is going to mean breaking off from the tech, because it's like any other transition,

'It's teatime in 20 minutes. We're having pancakes for pudding.

---

2   *Move Fast and Break Things: How Facebook, Google, and Amazon Have Cornered Culture and What It Means For All Of Us* (Macmillan, 2017).

Then you can go back on your tech.' You know the drill, because you've been managing transitions for years.

The thing with addiction, if that's what this is, is that in order to regulate ourselves and to have some ability to make decisions, we need a life outside of whatever it is that keeps drawing us in, something that is ultimately more attractive. A lot of the parenting around managing tech and the internet is about creating a real life outside of that and sometimes insisting that real life wins out. There are other parts of our young person's life where we have to act as their second brain; we help them remember things, make sure they are ready for school on time. I don't think it's that different for the tech question either and I think it's perfectly OK to insist that we all go out and do something together, get some fresh air, go away for a weekend, or go and eat some hideous take-away. I'm also a fan of The Tech Break.

Keeping an eye on our child's behaviour in the virtual world is not for wimps. Putting our heads in the sand and hoping for the best is not for wimps either.

Until it was no longer possible to do so, I kept an eye on what was going on online. I did it by keeping the login details so I could check. This might work for a bit, but you may quickly find that the child who can't tell the time or tie their own shoelaces is a master at getting around your carefully planned settings. It's another one of those bizarre aspects of parenting our children. If they allow us to check then that opens up the opportunity for conversations around what is sensible and interesting to post about yourself and how to respond to other people's posts. Then we can go on to talk about what it means to 'friend' someone and the difference between 'friend' and friend. (A lot) more on that later. We've had some good conversations around the sorts of things other children are posting and how they present themselves. It's important, I think, not to come over as completely negative about how young people communicate online, or we risk not being that person they would consider coming to when they are really in trouble. I've had to do a fair amount of: 'I worry about X, what she's wearing in those pictures and who those people are who are commenting.'

This can, I think, help our young people to think critically about what signals are sent out, even if they can't acknowledge how that applies to them. Of course if we're going to encourage critical thinking, we also have to admire and praise as well: 'That's a lovely picture.' Or suchlike.

When our children get their first smartphones or tablets, with internet access, it's perfectly reasonable for part of the package to be your right to check what they're up to from time to time. It's exciting to get your first phone, so we don't have to dump negativity all over that experience, but a conversation beforehand about regular checks being expected and the reasons why is, I think, necessary. It's up to you how often you check and how you do it. In my experience, the more explicitly you express that the better. Every evening, once a week, whatever. Something I learned is to expressly state when I was going to check the device, for example, 'I'm going to check in half an hour.'

I did most of my checks after bedtime, when the devices were downstairs.

The reasoning behind the warning is that we're not out to catch our children out, we're aiming for them to think hard about what it is they'd be comfortable with another person seeing and where they've over-stepped the mark. If our imminent check causes them to rapidly delete messages and posts, then so be it. We can always playfully drop in a remark way down the line: 'Looked like you were deleting a lot the other evening, what was that about?' For goodness sake, try to keep it light though.

What I found was that up to a point I was pretty good at

discovering online shenanigans (for instance Facebook being used in the browser instead of the app) and thank goodness I was. The things I've seen, the risks, the horror, the plans I've thwarted. Innocent child, how can you get yourself into these giant messes? It's almost like they've written on their social media profiles 'I'm really vulnerable, please exploit me'; only they can't see it and you are wrong and controlling because you are always wrong and controlling, about everything.

'But I know what I'm doing,' they may scream, right after posting a 'nude' to a 'friend' you're pretty sure is a 45-year-old paedophile.

Anyway (and breathe), I hope it doesn't come to that in your house. I don't recommend it as a carry-on.

There are plenty of resources[3] that may help get the message across about keeping safe online, without it coming from us. I relied on these on occasion and sometimes made watching them a condition of a person getting their device back after a misdemeanour. You may have a child who will fight you and every piece of advice every step of the way. My approach has been to battle on, because I have to trust that the advice goes in, on some level, even if I see little sign of it for a very long time. School can be another place for the message to be delivered and if you have a good working relationship with school you may be able to ask them to tackle particular topics. If the repercussions of unwise online activity play out outside the home, for instance if school or the police get involved in something, then they will be saying exactly what you have been. That's not a time for 'I told you so' but perhaps allow yourself that 'I told you so' look.

Increasingly and as our children get older you will lose

---

3   See www.nspcc.org.uk; www.thinkuknow.co.uk.

control over what they do online. They may have learned enough and be mature enough to conduct themselves safely, or they may not, in which case it's over to The School of Learning the Hard Way.

The Tech Break

You might already know how this goes.

A bigger than usual obsession takes hold, there's more secrecy, an escalation of behaviours, dysregulation, family life spirals downhill. You try to work out what is going on. You have a feeling in your gut that it's got something to do with happenings online. You may have more than your gut to go on. There may have been a complaint from a parent of another child at school or the police may have knocked on your door. You may have read and seen things you never imagined you would. Welcome to parenting in the internet age!

In my experience it's difficult if not impossible to introduce a tech break without bringing in shame. Sometimes, though, we have to be parents first and foremost, parents who keep our children safe and act in their best interests. And it's very likely that the shame is alive and well anyway and being held in.

Here's how it might go:

'I've noticed that things have got really difficult around here and I think it's got something to do with the internet.'

Cue howls of derision.

'You seem sad and anxious and it's not like you. I'm worried.'

Cue demonstrations of complete happiness, or a thud into anger.

I've found it's important not to bring in a sudden tech break ('sudden' is not a word that works well in any context in our house).

'We're going to have a break from the internet from bedtime tonight, for a week, and after that we'll see how things go.'

This is one of those stakes in the ground moments, when you have to absolutely hold the line. In my experience, once the fight is over, our child who was in an incredible mess online and who couldn't see how to free themselves from the situation they've got into, will be enormously relieved that we've stepped in. A peace may break out across your home that you had lost hope of ever experiencing again. You will be able to do things together like cook, paint, draw, watch Love Island and it will be enjoyable. This has played out many times in our house and the change in everyone's wellbeing will be so obvious that even our previously reluctant child will admit how lovely it is.

During a tech break, our child may seek us out more and need more of us. Attachment-seeking. It's golden time when we can fill them up with all the good nurture and acceptance and fun times and remind them that our reason for existence isn't just to stop them doing what they want to do. It is important during this time to talk about the online behaviours that caused the concern and to encourage some reflection. The magic car journey may be a good starting point for a non-confrontational exchange. I try to reiterate messages like: 'I'm doing my best to keep you safe, I'm not trying to be mean.'

The word 'safe' can, I think, be tricky, particularly if over-used, so I've had to grow my vocabulary a bit. Sometimes we may have to say it as it is: 'You are putting yourself at risk and it's my job to try to stop that happening.' 'You've broken the law and I'm going to do my best to make sure that doesn't happen again.'

Over-sharing

I'm old enough to remember when over-sharing meant entering into too much detail about one's toilet habits. Over-sharing has grown into something my simple, innocent mind struggles to comprehend.

Nudes and sexting

Apparently, everyone does it. Yes, they're all whipping down their pants, taking a snapshot and sending it to a friend. Don't panic, Mum! If not approving of sending 'nudes' or messages about particular sexual acts is a sign of being a dyed-in-the-wool, old-fashioned granny pants then I'm quite comfortable with that.

The slight difficulty, as you'll no doubt be aware, is that the friend who receives the 'nude' or the sext will then forward it on to many other friends, who will in turn send in on to their friends. It's like a hideously effective pyramid selling scheme.

'I only sent it to my boy/girlfriend,' our child may declare, as though that's all fine then. Of course the boy/girlfriend will shortly become an ex-boy/girlfriend, which then creates a whole other layer of reasons for hurt and vindictive sharing.

As they say, never send anything you're not prepared to see plastered on a banner alongside the main road into town. If only I had a fiver for every time I've said this.

Our young people, with their naivety, vulnerability and shaky attachments, appear to make these kinds of over-sharing mistakes more than their peers. And dysregulation, plus difficulties in understanding consequences, can make for a lot of trouble. Sending and sharing nude pictures, even having a nude picture on a device is, in the UK at least, against the law. It's a bit more serious than refusing to take your mum's advice to wear a coat on a freezing cold day.

And it may not be our young person that takes and sends a picture or a graphic message, it may be them encouraging others to commit the offence.

'Go on, send,' they may encourage another young person, over and over.

'Imagine their parents seeing that,' we may reason.

Reason. Logic. Consequences. Blah, blah, blah.

I've learned to approach the whole horrible subject of 'nudes' and sexting this way:

- Being clear that one does not send, keep or share a 'nude'. It's against the law. End of.
- Being clear that if you receive a 'nude', then you delete it straightaway. To do otherwise is AGAINST THE LAW.
- If it comes to light that nudes have been sent, kept or shared then access to devices, wifi, whatever will be removed.
- When other parents, school or the police get involved (or all three!) then my job is to keep the line, with empathy.
- Remind myself that learning the hard way can apply to absolutely everything, even when you think, 'Surely my child learned that lesson the last time.'
- Bolster up my coat of Teflon.
- Attempt a conversation, down the line, about what is private and the importance of respecting and valuing oneself.

In treading through this minefield, one of the biggest shocks for me was seeing the extent of the vulnerability laid out in black and white (and on occasion in hideous Technicolor). I can see the trauma and attachment difficulties laid bare (so to speak) but the law and other people don't. As far as we can control matters, I don't think our young people should have access to a technology that they can't yet cope with and that could land them with a criminal record or at the very least a warning that could well dog them for the rest of their already difficult years. And I know that leaves me swimming against an impossibly strong current.

Needy

Social media is full of young people expressing their need for attention, in concerning and messed-up ways. This is my opinion. I've seen many pictures of public sadness and pain, captioned with a meme designed to bring the concerned rushing in: tears flowing down cheeks, threats to self-harm and pictures of bridges.

'No one will miss me,' they post.

'Love you hun,' come the replies adorned with hearts.

'You don't know how bad I feel.'

'Always here for you babe.'

'No one understands.'

A lot of it is classic teenage drama, but some if it is more worrying. These conversations can go on for hours, with more and more participants being drawn in. Young people swim around the emotions of this and then maybe we call them down for tea, or ask them to bring their bath towel down, unaware of what's being played out.

I'm lucky, if that's the right word, that I have a number of young people in my life that show me the sorts of dramas that take place on social media. The vast majority of it doesn't take place in public spaces but via private messaging. I doubt that most parents have the faintest idea what their children are posting.

In my experience the best inoculation against all this is a close, accepting and enduring relationship in the family home. We've been able to have conversations around what 'neediness' online looks like and what might lie behind it.

'I wonder if that girl gets much attention at home,' you can enquire, even if it doesn't go anywhere.

'I hope you'd think about talking to me if you were that unhappy.'

There have been occasions when we've been able to laugh about someone's overwrought posts, because let's face it, teen angst does have its funny side. And there is an awful lot of social contagion about. That's not to say that there aren't situations when threats of self-harm shouldn't be taken seriously.

Do you actually know this person?

If your children are well into the teen years then I'll bet that you've uttered these words: 'Do you know this person in real life?'

It's far easier to make 'friends' online than in real life, especially for those of our young people who struggle with real-life peer relationships. But who are these friends? How well do you know them? How much are you willing to reveal about yourself to them?

For many teens, social media is a numbers game, the more friends the better. For many seemingly well-adjusted adults even, the same applies. A friend of a friend is still a friend, as is a friend of a friend of a friend. Look, I've got 500 friends! 'Well done,' we might say, 'but do you actually know any of them?' Because they are at the age when they move away from family into the influence of peers and because they may have zero risk awareness, our children will try to tell us that not knowing these people is perfectly fine because they are something even stronger than friends, they are 'mates' and they are 'all right'.

Maybe it's not such a big deal, but do we really know who sits behind the profiles? They might be legitimate, but what if they're not? Here are some things I've learned.

- Our children will have social media 'friends' with unclear intentions, and worse. While we may be able to spot them, our children almost certainly won't.
- Our children are likely to behave in ways that shouts their vulnerability from the rooftops.
- Our children may eschew all pleas from us that they keep their accounts locked down with privacy controls.
- Some of our children's vulnerability will lead them to seek meetings in real life, with virtual 'mates'.
- Shady characters, who may or may not have worrying intentions, can present themselves compellingly online. I don't think it's OK for our children to have long-running private conversations with strangers, no matter how well they may have wormed their way into our child's affections and if I discover any such goings on, I remove access. I'm mean like that.
- Strangers can become so attractive to our children that they will do almost anything to meet up with them. I learned to recognise the behaviours and the kinds of story telling that leads up to a meeting. On occasion I had to firmly say, 'No, you're not going out.' I know I failed to prevent one meeting and what led on from that was unbelievable and could have put the entire family at risk. This kind of thing does not happen in other families in the community in which I live.

- I had to set clear rules around going out in terms of knowing where I was dropping off and picking up and if it was at someone's house, then I would knock on the door and check. Sometimes me saying that I would knock on the door was enough to thwart the plan.
- Sometimes parents of friends of friends became, I think, too close for comfort, getting involved in online conversations and inviting groups of young people to stay over. We have some experience of collusive adults, a topic I cover in the 'Risk-Taking' chapter. For now, let's just say that it's been a big worry and something we've explored in open discussion in our family. Why would a parent want to be friends with their child's friends? Wouldn't you think it odd if I wanted to be friends with your friends? Yes, the answer is a massive big YES.

I don't want to pour a bucket of cold water over this communication revolution and come over too granny pants nanny state, but the design of social media is aimed completely and entirely at those with healthy attachments and without trauma histories, and even then it can present some major challenges. Many of our children, at the same time as being strongly attracted by social media, are just not ready for its nuances and its risks. They may do nothing so much as flush the toilet after a poo when we ask them to, but they can be manipulated into doing very risky things indeed by a stranger. And what's more, if we step in to keep them safe, they will hate us for it.

Some social media platforms all but do the job of groomers, sex offenders and drug dealers for them. I look at each new update with increasing incredulity. The latest, to one particular platform, particularly used by children, makes their actual, real-time whereabouts known to their followers. It's a brave new world, and one within which it is increasingly difficult to keep our children safe. Keeping them safe is, however, part of our job description, even if that makes us unpopular.

Selling

There are some aspects of early trauma that make you want to weep and for me this is one of them.

How do you get your hands on money when you find it difficult to save and you're dysregulated and your mum won't buy you whatever it is you so desperately want? The answer is you look around your room, you find something of value and you sell it. The internet allows you to not only sell your belongings, without question, but allows you to sell them to strangers, who you arrange to meet in real life to carry out the exchange. How the f**k did we get here?

I'd love to list you a whole series of tips, but I can't, other than if you suspect it's going on, hide away valuables and do what you can do prevent your child meeting up with a stranger, but you and I know that there's only so long we can hold this line. I think on balance it's probably best for us to try to release all emotional attachment to our child's belongings, even if it is a lovely watch that you bought them for their birthday. I thought perhaps I'd feel a strange relief once almost everything was gone. I don't.

The artist Michael Landy systematically destroyed all his belongings in an installation called Break Down. I hate that work.

Buying

What's the most bizarre item that's been delivered to your house? My friend Matthew took delivery of four inflatable boxing rings and a 3-D printer. I have intercepted a few classic purchases in my time, most of which ended up in the bin under the litter tray emptyings. Not the most therapeutic response, but my empathy dissolves when I unwrap elaborate smoking paraphernalia or worse.

I'm sure I don't need to point this out to you, but please do take extra measures to keep your credit and bank cards to yourself when these sorts of shenanigans are going on. Don't make online purchases when there are prying eyes in the room, don't save your card details on websites and gaming platforms and either keep your cards locked away or on your person at all times. Trauma might not be able to remember your birthday but that doesn't mean it doesn't know how to spend an awful lot of money on your credit card.

Drugs

Amongst the most concerning trade enabled by social media is in illegal drugs. It enables sellers to be matched with buyers and vice versa efficiently and quickly and it is awash with everything from cannabis to amphetamines to diazepam that are exchanged on city street corners and market town squares across the country. Educating ourselves about the social media enabled drug trade is our first line of defence. I've included more information in the chapter entitled 'The Hard Stuff', which refers to parenting and not the actual hard stuff.

CHAPTER 5

Family Life

A love of family life, in its broadest sense, is the reason most of us became therapeutic parents and it's got a lot to do with why many of our children, despite their poor early starts, go on to thrive. Family life: the things we do together, the shared jokes, the favourite days out and the memories, the stability are the glue that sticks us together. It also keeps the tank of good times topped up, which provides a buffer against the bad times.

Family life does of course mean different things in different families and different settings. It may mean five-hour round trips to top attractions, long-haul holidays and big family parties or it may mean something more low key. Either way is fine as long as it broadly works for everyone, including you.

Where we can come a cropper is when our expectations of family life come up against the realities of our family life. I've had to have a few stern words with myself along the way, but have a good idea now of what is fun and what definitely isn't fun. I've also got a lot more skilled at judging my energy levels and my mental capacity and throwing that into the equation, whenever the 'What are we going to do this weekend?' question comes up.

What shall we do this weekend?

That question can either bring on feelings of anticipated weekend fun or fill my head with rocks, depending on how things are. It's important to stress from the outset that during the difficult times it's perfectly fine to do absolutely nothing other than take care of ourselves. Just because other families are off doing exciting things, doesn't mean that we should feel we have to as well.

In our family, the answer to the 'What shall we do this weekend?' question may need the aid of a complicated set of algorithms in order to arrive at an answer. Some of the variables might be:

- Is a parent so livid with the actions of one of the children that they cannot possibly spend any quality time with them?
- Does the spell of a 'bad patch' need to be broken by some enjoyable, 'no matter what' time?
- When are our children likely to be out of bed by and what time does that nice cafe stop serving breakfast?
- Is anyone likely to be in a really tricky mood?
- What is the temperature outside and what are the chances of either (a) a coat being worn, or (b) sun tan lotion being applied?
- Are there any trigger-free films on at the cinema?
- Are there any outstanding local town council banning orders that may restrict plans?

When it is remarked upon that I am looking a little jaded, the requirement for complicated mental gymnastics such as this may partly explain why.

We have narrowed down the activities and the circumstances that work in our family and we're pretty good at this kind of complex decision-making now. Our over-riding aims of going out together are bonding, fun, nurture and acceptance. We should all feel better and more closely connected for having been out. It doesn't always work out that way, but that's the aim. There are a handful of tried-and-tested activities and we tend to rely on these. Sometimes we try something more adventurous and sometimes it works out and sometimes it doesn't.

Holidays

Holidays are a tricky business, aren't they? We've had some good getaways, we've also had some horrific ones. Most are a mixture of great days out and moments when I swear I will never go on another holiday again.

There may be some golden years, when our children are old enough not to drown in the pool or wonder off and get lost on a busy beach and yet still young enough to enjoy a bit of holiday fun. One thing's for sure though, even when our children are growing up, they may still find staying away from home very stressful and, like all stressful experiences, they probably won't be able to tell us they are stressed. The stress may materialise in all sorts of difficult ways and require top-quality therapeutic parenting, just when our brain is telling us it's gone on an extended vacation.

Our approach to holidays has been to learn what works and what doesn't and mostly not fiddle with the results too much. What has been a surprise is that just at the point we'd expected to be able to handle bigger holidays, we had to scale down and take things down a notch, reduce the travel time and stick to a few low-key favourites. This had a lot to do with increased pressure at school and the adolescent brain. It's been a time of reminding ourselves that it won't be like this forever.

There are a few alternatives to the big family holiday.

Mini-breaks

If a week or a fortnight away is too long, consider several long weekends. City breaks, a trip to a show or a concert, a caravan near a beach or a few days in a national park might all be an easier tasting menu of getaways.

Close to home

Staying an hour or two from home can allow for flexibility that long-haul holidays can't. Getting to your destination quickly and knowing that you can get home easily and under your own steam if it all goes wrong can just be the insurance policy required to help us through a long period together. Having an escape route might become increasingly important as our children get older and less (how can I put this?) amenable.

The Do It Yourself all-inclusive

This is a holiday I've invented, so, granted, it needs a bit of work but here's a rough description. Basically, you stay in a caravan or a house somewhere in walking distance of a number of pubs, other eating establishments and a small supermarket. For the duration of the holiday you do not cook, or do a 'big shop' and you barely wash up. This holiday came about because (a) we've always been able to eat out successfully and (b) every cell of my body was exhausted to the point of feeling tearful at the thought of heating up a pizza. It's not a cruise or an all-inclusive Club Med, but it can just take the pressure off for long enough to recuperate and remember what it is that you enjoy about each other's company.

The No Holiday

In many families there can be a stretch when our loved ones are too young to be left on their own but too old to want to come away on holiday with us, indeed some of us may have declared we will never leave our nearest and dearest alone in our house overnight, not never, ever, ever. I'm not saying that's me, you understand. If we find ourselves in this fix then it may be best to accept that we cannot go on holiday, for now. If this is the case, then save your money for the prolonged mega-holidays you're going to have when you have a break from 24/7 super-parenting.

The Quick Getaway

One child is going on a Geography field trip, the other is staying with a grandparent, the stars are in alignment and you have exactly two nights this year to escape. Do it. Get on that last-minute booking site and make the most of it. Go somewhere that won't be full of other people's children, go somewhere with comfortable beds and delicious food, go somewhere with a weak phone signal and no wifi. Refuel.

Festivities

The first Unofficial Guide included information about birthdays, Mother's and Father's Day and festivities such as Christmas, so I won't go over that ground again. It's enough to say that some of these family events may become a little easier over time and some may not. With age comes a growing ability to explore together what makes these times tricky and how they may be made easier to cope with. Our children should feel able to voice their feelings about, for example, Father's Day and to choose whether or how it is marked in our families. They may also benefit from sharing in the planning of, say, Christmas or other religious festivals. These are ways we demonstrate that we are in this business of family life together and their voice counts. That's not to say that sometimes we all have to go to things and take part in events that we would rather not, such as attending a family member's birthday fandango, but even then I would argue that concessions could be arrived at. It is however, in my opinion, not OK for someone to wreck the birthday fandango and then disappear off with mates for an evening of high jinx. Family life involves an amount of give and take. I realise this is easier theorised about than practised but it doesn't hurt to set a few expectations about what family life is about.

Relationships

Parenting traumatised, relationally damaged children has a brutal impact on our relationships with our partners, extended family and friends. Differences of opinion over parenting, exposure to prolonged stress, secondary trauma and isolation have a lot to answer for. Therapeutic parenting of all types shows you who your friends are and it will stress-test the strongest of relationships. I don't need to tell you that. You've got this far, so I'm guessing you'll know all about the relationships that trauma knocked on the head.

Marriages and partnerships

If I had a fiver for every time someone approached me with roughly this...

> 'My partner and I fall out over how to parent our child. I've been on a course about therapeutic parenting and I've read the books and it makes sense and it works. My partner won't go on any courses, tells me I'm being too soft and keeps intervening when I've got things under control and making things worse. It's really difficult at home and it's affecting our relationship.'

...I would be a rich woman.

I would also be a rich woman if I had a fiver for every time I've heard this...

> *'I do most of the chores around the house and I'm left to do all the parenting. My partner sits around a lot and hardly takes part in family life. I get that it's tiring being at work all day but I get no break from the children at all and I get no back-up when there's a conflict. I'm exhausted and feeling resentful.'*

I have also, dear readers, made exactly the same statements myself.

Raising averagely challenging children when you are in an averagely healthy relationship is, I'm told, do-able. You bumble on, brushing little things under the carpet, avoiding conflict or whatever and you get time together to remember what it is you love about each other. When raising our children, an averagely healthy relationship might not be good enough. Our children have a knack of spotting the fault lines in our relationships, working their little fingers in and pulling them apart. They may have experienced dysfunctional ways of doing relationships and feel safer when yours is dysfunctional too. Relational trauma requires relational repair[1] and that's absolutely true and it's true that the painful process of relational repair can be avoided if our families exist in relational chaos. Relational chaos keeps everyone's eyes away from where they really should be. If you are not yet in the depths of the teenage years then please trust me when I tell you that you will need the honesty, security and comfort of a good relationship more than you will ever imagine and if you fall out over whether the children are allowed to drink Coke or eat with their elbows on the table or you argue over who's going to take

---

1   *Working with Relational and Developmental Trauma in Children and Adolescents*, Dr Karen Treisman, Routledge, 2016

the rubbish out or sort the whites from the colours then you may find what's coming very difficult to negotiate indeed.

I am no relationship guru and so I hesitate to offer advice, but I will share with you what I have learned and I think it's best that I do that without pulling any punches.

Therapy and therapeutic parenting

It is crucial, in my opinion. that both partners do at least some therapeutic parenting training together, in the same room (the clue here is in the word 'partner'). Travel there together, work out what you want help with, nod and make eye contact when you hear something that makes complete sense, comfort each other when it all gets a bit too much. There will be lots of reasons why it is difficult to clear a few days to go to training or therapy together but it will reap rewards way into the future. You are on a long and potentially treacherous journey and it is better, in my experience, if you take that journey together, sharing the light-bulb moments, working through strategies together, sharing the load. It is perhaps inevitable that one of you is going to be ahead of the other in terms of the understanding and practice of therapeutic parenting. That's just the way it is. Whichever one of you is a bit ahead will have to accept that their partner is going to take a bit more time to get it and to help them along. The one taking a bit more time must accept that their partner might be on to something and isn't just indulging in hours of training and education for the hell of it. It's tempting to get locked into right and wrong, hard and soft and play out long-lasting power struggles. There will be no winners and the biggest losers of all will be our children, caught in the crossfire.

Coming together when we are on different therapeutic pages is about courageous amounts of honesty and compassion. We go into denial about the benefits of therapeutic parenting because let's face it, we all wish that the simple, traditional methods worked because it would make our lives massively easier. But they don't. I think it's OK to voice this kind of thing. I also think it's OK to admit that we find it so very difficult and that it runs so much against the grain that we want to pretend it's all a pile of snowflake, liberal crap.

'I find it difficult to get my head around.'

'I really struggle when he just doesn't do what I tell him to do.'

'I never did anything like that when I was a child.'

These are all perfectly acceptable starting points, to be shared, in the spirit of connecting with each other's struggles.

'It makes me so angry when she takes food.'

'I can't bear the chaos.'

'When he got angry I reacted really badly.'

'I'm mortified he did that.'

Exposing ourselves with honesty is only possible if we feel accepted by our partners in all our glorious and imperfect humanity. So, my friends and fellow travellers, start sharing your triggers and Red Buttons with each other, share your hopes and dreams and mourn the broken ones together, talk through the strategies that work and that don't, feel empathy for each other and encourage each other to feel empathy for your children. Try really hard not to blame each other when something doesn't go to plan and create the environment where you can talk through what you should have done differently. Tomorrow is a new day.

Mr D and I went through some rough times, especially when

things at home were fighty and scary. It's difficult to maintain any kind of positive relationship with anybody when you are being regularly triggered into your own fight/flight/freeze responses. We were in fight a lot of the time and with that comes unkind words, lack of thought and general reactivity. There were times when I had to physically hold back my own flight response (handbag, car keys, Travelodge website) and we both had prolonged periods of numbness and what you could call dissociation and secondary trauma. We were in a state of grief, shock and denial and what better way to deal with these bastards than to take our pain out on each other? Empathy didn't get a look-in for a while.

Things are very different now and that's mainly because we talk about this stuff. We share what we find difficult and triggering and accept that our difficulties and triggers are not the same. We accept that we can both behave abominably just as we can both remain calm in the most horrific situations. It's important, I think, to remember that we are both fallible and doing our best, to play to each other's strengths and to take care of each other. We've ended up in a kind of rhythm where when one of us takes an emotional dive, the other rises to take the strain and vice versa. And we can both rant and rage to each other and be supremely untherapeutic, without fear of criticism. For us it's a kind of safe space. There needs to be somewhere to put those really dark and murderous thoughts that we all have from time to time, without fear of being hauled in front of a Child Protection Panel. I told Mr D about a time I got so close to punching someone that my fists were itching with the strain of not punching that person. His response, 'I know EXACTLY what you mean' was perfect. I mimed the punch, well, several punches, with sound effects and swearing and felt a bit better for it. The important part of that story is that I had someone I could tell, someone who didn't panic and who didn't call in Child Protection. We all need that someone because sometimes traumatised young people can take us to psychological places we never knew existed.

Sharing the load

School runs, clubs, bedtimes, washing-up, laundry, remembering everyone's birthdays, when teacher training days are and the brand of cheddar that is acceptable to the majority of family members are all chores that someone has to carry out. They are boring and take up space in our frazzled brains. They are even more boring and frazzling when they are not shared equally and let's face it, it's not that uncommon for one partner to do an awful lot more than the other (yes, I'm talking to you, Fixy and Avoidance). I hear this from most of my friends to varying degrees. (I'm told it's to do with their mothers who treated them like princes or princesses, but I'm not going there.) In average families I guess this could be averagely annoying and involve average disagreements about who should do more, averagely bad atmospheres and stand-offs. In our families I'm not sure it's that simple.

In our families there are many extra responsibilities that couldn't even be classed as boring because they are too demanding to be boring. I'm thinking of things like policing fights between siblings, working out who's stolen what from whom, mending broken things, being assessed, going to tribunals, going to therapy and rewriting life story books. If you don't partake in many of the chores or extra responsibilities and you don't have a good reason for your lack of involvement (extreme illness, living on another continent) then you need to do your fair share. There's no fluffy way of putting this. Get up off of that sofa, put on some good music and get those washing-up gloves on. Therapeutic parenting is no place for shirkers.

Now and again you may need to say, 'I need help', rather than seethe and fling the vacuum cleaner around. Or you may need to notice that help is needed and step in. For a longer-term peace accord it may be useful to list out the chores and share them out. Or you might need to buy a dishwasher and sub-contract out some of the chores. Di and Amanda, who clean our house once a fortnight, keep it habitable enough that friends can call around without having to give a day's notice and they are a lot cheaper than a divorce. I wish I'd met Di and Amanda years ago, but even if I had, Captain Fixy may still have got in the way.

Time for each other

I might pick up a magazine or a Sunday supplement and read about how to keep one's marriage sweet by going on date nights, mini-breaks and having romantic meals and couple's massages. The accompanying stock photo will be a fresh-looking couple holding hands over a candle-lit dinner or indulging in a playful pillow fight. I can't remember the last time I had a pillow fight. This kind of guff is just that, guff, and no one lives like this; however, many of us really, really don't live like this. For instance, I know people who can go out for the evening and leave their teenage children at home. I know! Imagine that. They can go out for meals with friends, watch grown-up films, get a couple's massage. Many of us have few to zero babysitting options when our children are children and when they become teenagers the problem may get worse. Yeah, I know, it's not what we hoped for, is it? The Babysitting Gap is that period between babysitting no longer being an appropriate thing because of biological age (at its most extreme the babysittee is older than all available babysitters) and the capability of our lovelies to be left alone. It's that difference between biological age and developmental age thing. In my experience The Babysitting Gap lasts for a long time and makes carving out time for each other rather difficult.

If you find yourselves in The Babysitting Gap then you will have to grab opportunities where you can and be much more creative than your friends have to be. Mr D and I have got quite good at this. We know how long an adolescent weekend lie-in lasts and have worked out what we can squeeze into that time. It's nothing amazing. We dropped our expectations years ago, but let me tell you that a walk across the fields to the garden centre cafe is pretty blissful when you've been out together as infrequently as we have. Sometimes we make it across the fields into a cafe in town. That's something I'd wake up feeling excited about. There are a few places we stay overnight if the opportunity arises. These venues aren't too far away (who wants to waste precious hours travelling?) and are reliably nice, with good food. It's not a romantic weekend in Salzburg but it works for us.

Despite all the pressures our relationship has come under, it is good and strong. I think it may be stronger for having had to limber up and rise to the challenge.

It goes without saying that all the honesty, compassion and kitchen gadgetry in the world will not be enough to save some partnerships and that not all partnerships should be saved. If you love your partner though and you want to imagine a life together once the most intense of your therapeutic parenting years are over then value and take care of each other in all your wonderful and imperfect glory.

Extended family and friends

Some get it, some don't get it, some think they get it but they don't, some we just couldn't do without, others disappear without trace. You will know as well as I do that trauma doesn't just test our partnerships and marriages, it tests all our relationships and some of them break.

Get Its

Hooray, someone close to us gets it. They intrinsically accept us and our families as we are and they take us as the full package of up, down, optimistic, pessimistic, fun and complete drag. Value them, love them, talk to them and let them help.

Don't Get Its

Some Don't Get Its eventually do, and it will be worth chipping away and bringing them alongside. Beware of taking on too much of the responsibility for doing this though. Don't Get Its are easier if they don't vocalise their not getting it too often. If they do vocalise and the effect of that is to leave you feeling like a broken failure then you will have to spend less time with them, or kindly suggest to them they are going to have cut out the parenting lectures. Maintaining good relations in battlefield conditions can have a lot to do with keeping one's mouth shut, but not at the expense of our wellbeing and mental health. Family and friendship dynamics can be difficult to negotiate, even at the best of times; they can be close to impossible when times are so hard you find yourself on the edge of coping. The years of adolescence can be particularly testing of family bonds. It might be that cutipops is no longer so cute and the wool is pulled away from everyone's eyes. 'I see what you've been on about all this time,' they say and you will have to smile and try hard not to retort, 'I told you so'. Or cutipops may become so uncute that they become a serious challenge to the Don't Get Its who may provide you with sterner lectures than you've had to put up with before or who alternatively may absent themselves from your lives.

I'm a firm believer in maintaining relationships if at all possible and loving and valuing people for who they are and not trying too hard to wish they were someone else. Having said that, standing on the front line of trauma means sometimes having to make difficult decisions. If the only reason that a relationship is still limping on is because you give and give and make allowances and keep your mouth shut and privately rage, then maybe it's time to put the relationship out of its misery, or at least put it in the deep freeze for a while.

The Disappeared

I've been lucky not to have too many Disappeareds in my life but I know some who can count some previously close and valued relationships amongst their disappeared. It's painful and sad when those we banked on to be alongside us can't, for whatever reason, last the course. We stitch our children into our bodies and minds and that act of love and union renders some relationships void. Despite the sadness there's also a release. You no longer have to be the person straining to bridge two sides of an ever-widening ravine.

The good news

Some relationships no longer fit, we grow out of them, or they become too flimsy. Every relationship that drifts away leaves us with space: space to work out who we are and who we want to accompany us on this long-distance march. It's like clearing out our wardrobes of clothes we don't wear any more. We make space to go shopping.

It can take some courage to get back out into the world so go gently if you need to. Support groups, including online groups, can be a good way of making connections with those who will 'get it' for sure. We need other (trauma-free) relationships too because if you're anything like me you'll need reminding that there is a life beyond trauma. I've found new friendships in the most unlikely places and these are taking my life in new and exciting directions it wouldn't otherwise have gone in.

CHAPTER 6

Risk-Taking

Whenever I consider the potential vulnerabilities of the adolescent brain in terms of risk-taking I am struck by how many of these are pre-existing vulnerabilities in young people with attachment difficulties and early life trauma. It's the risk icing on top of the risk drizzle cake.

Looking on the bright side, if any group is practised at parenting impulsive children who have difficulty predicting consequences or learning from mistakes or who favour a bit of authority-bashing then that's us. We've grabbed our children before they've run into traffic, or into the arms of a stranger, we've cajoled and convinced them to wear cycle helmets and sunscreen, we've nursed them after they've eaten all the biscuits, we've picked up the pieces after they've sworn at a teacher and what's more we've kept them alive all this time. Some of us may even conclude we've been parenting mini-adolescents all along. We've got this.

Attraction to risk

Something I hear over and over from therapeutic parents is this: 'My child will gravitate to the one child in the class that brings out the worst in them.'

Risky children find other risky children. It's uncanny. It's like they have little search-and-locate radars on-board. Some of our children learn that although it can be fun choosing to go running about with the other running-about children, that choice might result in them getting into trouble more often and being ostracised by the other children. Sometimes it can be difficult for them to learn these lessons as perhaps the attractions of running about are too strong to resist or getting into trouble reinforces how they already feel about themselves, or they just don't have any other friends to fall back on and to have a running-about friend is better than having no friend at all.

This kind of dynamic in the junior school playground is one thing, at secondary school, college, out in the street and on social media it can be a whole other thing. For those of us lucky enough to have been raised by safe and caring adults who demonstrated who to be wary of and who gave us a strong and cohesive sense of ourselves and our self-worth, spotting the running-about types is probably relatively easy. When I walk through town I am subconsciously clocking a person's state of dress, their cleanliness, their body language, gait, the volume of their voice, whether they are behaving in a way that draws attention, how they make me feel. It doesn't take that much to fire off my 'pay attention' warning system, my 'give this person a wide berth' and my 'definitely no eye contact' responses. I see the vast majority of other people respond in exactly the same way to the same cues. What I notice in some of our young people is great skill in noticing the cues, but an entirely different response to a person presenting themselves as potentially risky.

Witnessing a young person moving towards instead of away from risky individuals is unsettling and concerning. Whilst we may understand some of the underlying historical reasons (perhaps they learnt to keep themselves safe by keeping danger close), seeing this vulnerability and perhaps even feeling at risk ourselves because of it is something most parents never have to experience.

'It's fine, Mum, he's my mate, you'd like him,' is little comfort when all of your brain is screaming, 'Get away now, danger, danger, danger'.

If we parent children with faulty danger systems then we must, for as long as we possibly can, act as their proxy danger system. We must verbalise how we keep ourselves safe by saying things like, 'I didn't like the look of that person who was skulking around the underpass, something wasn't right.' And we verbalise why we wanted to have the conversation once we were well away from the dodgy person by the underpass.

We must also make executive decisions about where our children go and who with, when we have the opportunity to. We might limit time spent with friends if we know that an hour is far more likely to be successfully managed than two or four hours. You might say that you will only drop your child at someone's house, once you've spoken to their parent or carer. None of these measures, as I'm sure you will already know, will mitigate against our dearest children taking the most horrific risks. The most determined will find a way of escaping the reaches of your threat detection system.

This is one of those aspects of parenting that requires we stand up and be counted. Keeping vulnerable children safe is no job for the cowardly or the theoretical and I honestly think that most people who've never had to do it, have very little idea how difficult it is. It's excruciatingly, frustratingly difficult and it's laden with impossible decisions, huge demands and it can feel like a massive exercise in lose–lose. If you fail to keep them safe, then it's a clear lose and if you keep them safe, they hate you for it. And, the loser's icing on the loser's cake is when we find ourselves accused of being too strict and controlling in meetings, around tables, where minutes are being taken. Give me a break.

The following broad and sweeping categories are probably judgemental and discriminatory. I don't care so spare me the inclusivity lecture. These are some of the types that you may find your children and young people are drawn to.

Neglectful, chaotic families

In her book, *The Teenage Brain*,[1] Frances E. Jensen says:

> One thing I learned as a parent of teenagers is that while you can try to set your own tone in your own household, you are really sharing parenting with all the parents of your kid's friends – adults you might not have otherwise chosen to be intimate role models for your kids.

She describes a dad who provided beer at his teenaged son's party. I wish that was what kept me awake at night.

While it might be fine for our children to knock about with their friend at school, at the park or at your house, when they ask to go to their house, or even stay for a sleepover and you know or at least strongly suspect what that would entail, that's when things can get very difficult indeed. It's up to you, of course it is, and you may not choose to fight every battle and it may depend on your child's age, but if a house clearly isn't safe and if there are unsafe adults around, then I really believe it is our job to step in and carefully wrap up the 'NO', perhaps without using the 'NO' at all.

---

1   Frances E Jensen, MD, with Amy Ellis Nutt, *The Teenage Brain* (Thorsons, 2015).

> *'Not this time but you could invite your friend to stay here if you like.'*

> *'I'm sorry, we're already planning to* <insert something equally as exciting>*.'*

If it's at all possible, I think it's worth attempting a conversation about what you perceive as the risks and the dangers you wouldn't want your child exposed to because you love them and care about them. It's crucial though not to criticise the friend or to be disparaging about their family. Our adolescents are naturally moving away from us and towards their peers and may feel an extra level of responsibility and protection towards them, especially if they are living in circumstances similar to those our child left behind in their birth family. It may be useful to explore the worries your child has about their friend and to share in their concern. It's our old friend empathy in action.

Collusive adults

A collusive adult is the parent of a child who suddenly becomes a best friend out of nowhere, or maybe the aunt or uncle of the mate of someone's mate (it's likely to be hazy). What I've learnt about collusive adults, having never previously been aware of their existence, is that they enjoy being around teenagers, but not in a healthy way. They treat young people as if they were their own friends, they 'friend' them on social media and they message them and other children and they get embroiled in and fuel the teen dramas. They are also incredibly permissive, so it's brilliant fun to stay at their house and they have absolutely no boundaries. They are like child-adults and will view you, an adult-adult, with great suspicion. It will be difficult to work out where they live, so you may have to be a super-detective as well as super-parent.

Some of them may present better than you'd think, but the signs will be there. They will try to swallow up your child like a giant marshmallow. They are very likely to have their own attachment and trauma histories but that really isn't our responsibility. I may be stretching this a bit, but the one good(ish) thing about collusive adults is that they don't seem to stay on the scene for too long.

Your weapon against collusive adults is modelling adult behaviour, calmly and confidently.

> 'I wonder how you would feel if I "friended" your friends and messaged them in the middle of the night?'

> 'I know you'd rather I was more fun like X is but I don't think the rest of our family would like it if I invited loads of random kids to sleep in our house. In fact I don't think you'd like it.'

> 'Our house is somewhere we are all safe.'

Criminals

The friend whose dad can always get you what you want, no questions asked, the friend who steals from shops, the older kids who can spot a vulnerable younger person a mile off, the drug dealers, the groomers, the gangsters, the traffickers. When you live a relatively normal life, you don't see the scummy underbelly of society. When you parent vulnerable adolescents you may if you're unlucky see a part of society that will change you forever. Some of our young people seem to explore and experience a level of risk that would be intolerable to us, need to really feel the full force of that risk before they find their own level of unbearable and pull back. I don't know whether there is anything we can do to influence that level; I suspect that there isn't.

When our children are younger, we do everything in our

power to keep them safe and away from such criminal types. We open up conversations about risk and we practise curiosity. When we can no longer do this, when our young people are hell-bent on following their risk radars, when no amount of threatening, reasoning or encouraging works then we are left with few options.

You'll see the signs that they are running about with unsavoury types. They may become more than usually cocky, have access to money and expensive items that can't be explained and they may refuse to tell you where they're going and come home late or not at all, with no reasonable explanation. The secrecy is because they know we won't approve and deep down they know we are right not to approve and they would feel terribly unsafe if we did.

My advice is this:

- Make keeping everyone else in your family safe your priority.
- Consider changing your locks.
- Keep money, bank cards and details locked away.
- Take extremely good care of yourself.
- Ready yourself for the long haul.
- Be mindful of your stakes in the ground, your no negotiation boundaries and be prepared to call the police if you need to.
- Try to stay connected with your young person even if this is only possible remotely and digitally.
- Pay extra special attention to siblings who will also be unsettled by the proximity of risk.

Our young people may get a nasty taste of risky individuals and 'bounce back' to us. We may never find out what's happened but we become skilled at knowing that something has. When they bounce back, they are going to try as hard as they can to hide their need for reassurance and comfort. They might be rude and stroppy but I still think it's important to accept them back, for safety's sake and because we are the adult and we know they may have taken a terrible risk and they need us. You may have been sick with worry, but a cup of coffee, a bowl of soup and a film will speak volumes more than, 'Where the hell have you been?!' The maxim 'think toddler' works well into adolescence.

The ladder of risk

If you have a child who insists on climbing the ladder of risk and rebellion then you will know better than me that there are many different routes up the ladder. Here's an example.

cocaine
↑
ecstasy
↑
cannabis
↑
alcohol
↑
tobacco
↑
vapes
↑
energy drinks
↑
chewing gum

How high up the ladder our children end up climbing is anyone's guess. Let's just say that I've observed a steadfast march to the top of several and it's only now that I can see where it started and that there was probably very little I could have done to encourage the ladder to be descended. I hope I'm not being too opaque. This, as you will appreciate, is a sensitive subject.

When our little children come to us, with their need for control and their suspicion of adults, we have a battle on our hands to prevent them choking on chewing gum or consuming gallons of caffeinated fizzy drinks before bedtime. It's our job to steer them away from these things when they are little and it's their job to fight us every step of the way. But it's one thing sneaking some dinner money to buy a can of Red Bull, it's quite another drinking yourself into oblivion or taking so much ecstasy you risk having a heart attack. There may not be too much distance between spending a tenner on pick-and-mix and eating until you throw up and consuming dangerous, life-threatening amounts of drugs. The 'stop' button may take a long time to come on line and while it's taking its time the parenting ride can become very perilous indeed.

My advice, back to myself as the parent of younger children, is to lighten up about chewing gum, energy drinks, vapes and probably tobacco. The writing was on the wall from the start and some of the verve and gusto in climbing the ladder was fuelled with my disapproval of this relatively harmless consumption. In many ways, my disapproval of something pretty much guaranteed it would be tried. I still remember a special assembly at school about the dangers of the over-consumption of energy drinks and the newly introduced school ban. There could not have been a better advert for energy drinks. (And before you write me a furious letter about the dangers of smoking tobacco, I know, but there comes a time when things become relative.)

Some of our children are particularly vulnerable to the delights of highly risky substance consumption or other very risky involvements. As I mentioned, their need for control and their suspicion of adult advice is enough of a starting point. As they grow older they may find themselves part of dysfunctional peer groups and their desire to 'fit in' may make it difficult if not impossible for them to say 'no' and walk away from the group. If they can't hear 'no' from us, their ever-loving parents then I suspect it is difficult for them to say it to themselves. As I've described in other chapters, there may be times when we have to stand up and say a very firm 'no', despite their protestations and threats. 'It's my job to keep you safe,' may not wash now, but I think it still bears repeating, because somewhere along the line, it goes in.

I like a metaphor and at the risk of stretching the ladder metaphor to breaking point, I'll share with you how I think of myself when someone is waving around on the top of the ladder, acting like an idiot. I imagine myself at the bottom, in my garden, getting on with garden-y jobs, enjoying the sunshine and I say to myself, 'When it's time for you to come back down, I'll be here, waiting for you.'

Sex

We'd probably all like to think our young people will wait for the right person to come along before embarking upon a sexual relationship, after having made a considered decision about the right contraception to use. In reality our young people with their relational difficulties, their difficulties predicting consequences and the extra adolescent bits on top (impulsivity, sensation-seeking) are at least as likely as their peers to rush into sexual relationships unwisely and for the wrong reasons.

We can try to offer advice but really, who wants advice about sex from their parents? Certainly not our kids. My approach has been, excuse the pun, quick in and quick out. Short pieces of advice, backed up by sex education at school. Schools get a lot of criticism for their openness about sex and the access they provide to contraception but I say bring it on.

Here's the approach I took, over many years, in an effort to instil awareness of power, consent and responsibility in sexual relationships.

Whether our young people like it or not, the law is clear about under-age sex, even if in practice things are less clear. This can be a minefield for our less emotionally mature young people who may gravitate towards friends and partners who are younger than they are. The consequences of being reported by a parent, carer, or teacher for having a sexual relationship with a minor can be serious and whilst it's true that many under-16s are involved in sexual relationships ('Everyone's doing it, Mum'), they may be conducting themselves with more subtlety than our young people are capable of. I think we must have these conversations frankly and openly, even if we know it won't change the course of events right now.

We've talked about bodies and sexuality in the context of music videos and advertising and, without wanting to come over as a complete prude, this can be a good way of exploring how we present ourselves, the messages we send out and unrealistic images of beautiful, sexy people and disempowering gender stereotyping.

Young people with low self-esteem and self-respect of course don't think they are worth much. It's sad when you see this playing out. Conversations about valuing oneself, being choosy who we enter into relationships with and ways in which we can claim and assert ourselves in relationships are worth having.

Consent isn't only about consent to sex, it's about who we allow to touch us and how that touch feels. Some of our young people may still be struggling with sensory issues around touch, and conversations about what constitutes consent and appropriate and inappropriate touch can, I think, help our young people to think critically and pro-actively. If we can, we must share our own experiences of inappropriate touch and how it made us feel. The line I've gone with is 'If it feels wrong, it is wrong.' We want our young people to feel empowered in all their relationships.

Whether you allow your young person to have sex in your house or not is a personal matter and I don't think it's anyone else's business. Decide on your house rules and stick to them and don't be swayed by 'Well, they could be doing it in the woods, at the back of Tesco, anywhere.' So be it. Plus, there may be younger siblings at home, which can put a different spin on things.

If your young person is sexually active then the priority of course has to be contraception. You and I may get the consequences of unprotected sex, but our consequence-lacking loved ones won't ever think it will happen to them. It's tough but taking them to the clinic, without judgement, may be the best we can do. I haven't had to do that so I can't say how I would find it. I hope I manage to maintain emotional connection because this is what may enable our advice to be taken or at the very least our offer of a lift to be accepted. There's a lot to be said for not being shocked and my experiences have set me up better for not being shocked about sex, than for instance not being shocked about drug use.

If you suspect that your child is being sexually exploited then go to the CEOPS website for information[2] and inform your social worker and the police, if necessary in writing. Sexual exploitation is rare in the general population but sadly some of our young people are particularly vulnerable in this respect and as we've learned from recent investigations those seeking

---

2   www.ceop.police.uk.

to groom young people are skilled at identifying and targeting the most vulnerable. If you suspect your child is being targeted then I'll make no bones about it, you are their best protection: because you care, because you worry about where your child is, because you act when you need to and because you hold their wellbeing at the heart of your family life.

Natural consequences and risk

It's only in recent years that I've heard the phrase 'natural consequences', I guess because before becoming a therapeutic parent consequences were just that, consequences. There was no getting around them.

The most baffling aspect of being a therapeutic parent for me has been that consequences, the thought of them, or the actual things themselves, don't or at least rarely change behaviour. The natural laws of the universe, the land and society are there to be proven wrong, fought against, argued with. They can't be accepted, because that would just be way too easy.

When our children are little, we may spend an awful lot of energy protecting them from natural consequences and from convincing them that they even exist. We make them wear armbands in the deep end of the swimming pool, we force them to drink, we stop them from putting their hands into the mouths of dogs. We do this to keep them alive and we are able to do this primarily because we are bigger than they are. Forcing them to do things to prevent them from dying or being seriously maimed turns us, in their eyes, into the bad guys. It's a lose–lose situation. Be the good guy and your child ends up in hospital with an infected dog bite (they also refused to let you wash the wound), protect your child from injury and they hate you for it. If I had to boil therapeutic parenting down, that would pretty much be it.

Fast forward to adolescence and we have a problem on our hands. For one, life's risks become that bit riskier; for two, we have lost our height advantage; and for three, that darned adolescent brain.

The adolescent brain is not that great at looking ahead, making predictions about what might happen if, and it's got the taste for risk. Sounds a lot like the traumatised brain, doesn't it? Double whammy!

I'm going to go on and talk about what is great and liberating about embracing natural consequences in the chapter 'Toolbox of Techniques'. I am generally a fan of natural consequences when it comes down to things like getting a bit cold, or hungry, or tired because of refusal to dress properly, eat, sleep, whatever. I'm even quite a fan of some school consequences, within reason. And I don't mind a bit of social consequence ('My friend isn't speaking to me', 'Has that got anything to do with you being an hour late to meet them yesterday?' 'I hate you'). However, I don't really enjoy anything much about criminal consequences, horrible injury consequences, coming down from drugs consequences, losing your job consequences.

It's all well and good having a young child who 'can't do consequences', but many of our big, teenaged, toddler boys and girls crash into the wider world incredibly under-equipped to deal with its boundaries, its norms and its rules. Basically they learn the hard way, or they don't learn at all. This is why I am a fan of ushering in careful, natural consequences when our children are younger. Some of that learning goes in and will, we hope, start to make sense once they hit the hard brick wall of the real world.

As therapeutic parents, who care deeply for our children and who worry every single day about their safety, life chances and happiness, there are a narrow range of strategies open to us. It is very important that we use them.

The primary strategy is to pick up the pieces after a natural consequence has played out and the dust has settled. It's tempting when, let's say, your strapping teen has broken a bone from doing something ridiculous, to deliver the 'I told you so' message of condolence. We have to save that reflex to share with our friends in the pub as a way of letting off steam, but it's important I think not to let it leak out in front of our suffering child. Pain, either physical or emotional, can bring our child back to us to seek nurture and comfort. These are times we can use to great therapeutic advantage.

'You must be in so much pain.'

'Here is some paracetamol and a hot chocolate.'

'Let's sit and watch a film.'

'Tell me about it.'

'I can understand why you did that, I'm sad you're hurting because of it though.'

There may be opportunity to explore what happened and how things could have gone differently. I think that kind of replaying can be quite powerful. It can reframe a terrible incident and help to develop predictive skills. We want to arm our children with the ability to stop and ask themselves the 'what if?' question, not to shame them into further proving they are a hopeless case. There are times when we have to carry on believing, even when they have lost hope.

We may find ourselves having to pick up the pieces once the police are involved with something. I hope you don't find yourself doing that, because it's not what we ever hoped for family life. I have found the police to be refreshing in their approach to consequences. They set them out in a no-nonsense, firm but kind way. There's no wriggling out of a consequences with a copper. The 'but but but' doesn't work and the officers I've had the pleasure of meeting have been skilled at not getting derailed by the wave of illogical excuses that can knock me off my feet and drag me under. It's partly because they're not emotionally entangled like I am. And they are used to this kind of thing.

There may come a time when our beloved young people rush at risk with such gusto and a blindness to the consequences that there is nothing more we can do than occasionally express our concern and let events take their course. We will lie awake night after night consumed by a worry that we wish our young people could feel just a tiny amount of. They may be acting as though they are invincible, as though nothing and no one can touch them. It's terrifying and I can't pretend otherwise. One hopes that sooner or later they will recall us having patiently blown up their water wings in the swimming pool changing rooms.

I'll wrap up again with a short lecture about self-care. If our loved ones find themselves racing off, playing roulette with risk, then there comes a time when we have to let them take that part of the journey for themselves. We have no choice, because part of that journey is about being in opposition to us. The more we tell them not to do whatever it is, the more they will. It's teenage rebellion turned up to MAX. As they learn about consequences the hard way and discover how far they are going to travel along the Rue de Self Destruction, we must use this time to repair and rebuild ourselves. It'll be self-care on a level we've never had to practise at before. We may even have to rediscover who we are, what we like about ourselves, what are talents are. It's not a selfish act. We deserve to be healthy and whole and when our young people return to us, bearing the scars and the learning of whatever it is they've exposed themselves to, they will find us calm and confident and living a full life that they desire to play a part in. That's the aim, anyway.

CHAPTER 7

Education

I have yet to meet a therapeutic parent who reports that their child's experiences of school have been wonderful, miraculous and life-affirming. Perhaps I just haven't met the right parents. What seems to be emerging though, in England at least, is that looked-after and previously looked-after children are more likely than their peers to be excluded from school and perform less well than their peers in exams.

Whilst we can campaign for the changes to education that would benefit our children and hope for better, many of us are left having to make the best of what's on offer. We have a right to shop around to find the school that will be the best fit and that's exactly what we should do. Whether a school approaches our child with knowledge and acceptance of the challenges they face, or a muscular determination to make them better, has a direct and significant impact on their wellbeing and ultimately on their achievement and future. It also has a strong knock-on effect on the whole family.

The good news is that since I stepped rather naively through the gates of our first school, things have moved on significantly. The words 'attachment', 'trauma' and 'care-experienced' can be used without fear of being met with sighing and eye-rolling. Governments are promoting the needs of adopted and care-experienced children and are getting better at tracking their attainment. I know that if your child's needs are not being met in their school and you are struggling to be heard, it will feel as though nothing has changed. What I'm going to try to do in this chapter is to help you harness the information and energy that's out there and use it to arm yourself to challenge and influence your child's education in a way that doesn't leave you and the school at loggerheads. It's one more thing we have to take on as therapeutic parents, alongside all the other things, and I dream of a time when our tired bodies and brains don't have to rise to the occasion. But if there's one aspect of our child's success and wellbeing we can usefully focus our energies on, it's school. School has a huge influence on our children, for good, or not so good, so come on, let's get this sorted.

Choosing a school

In my previous *Unofficial Guide* I went into some detail about what to look out for when choosing a school for our children. I won't regurgitate all that here because you've invested good money in this book and you'll be looking forward to leaving debates about dark cloud and rainbow behaviour systems and golden time behind. I will highlight the aspects of school that I think it's important to consider when selecting a secondary or high school.

All of this of course pre-supposes that there is a choice. We don't all live within easy distance of a number of schools. I don't, but I have learned that it is important to at least consider schools that are not on our doorstep, if that means our child can go somewhere they are more likely to flourish. Long commutes and expensive transport are hits that we may have to consider taking (yes, I know).

Think about the challenges that your child will set their school. Are they likely to have difficulties sitting still for long periods? How are they in large, busy groups? How well organised are they? What is the likelihood they will kick against rules? Are they compliant at school but then come home and spill trauma everywhere? Are they overly anxious about meeting deadlines? What is their level of need for safety? Would they like a wide-open campus, or would they fare better with something more contained? Are they likely to school refuse? Do they need time out for appointments, including recovery time? When we assess a school for suitability, we're assessing it against the specific needs of our child. We need a specification.

Look around as many schools as you can with your specification in mind. As well as considering how a school could meet the needs of your child, ask yourself what the atmosphere is, what your gut tells you. Do you feel welcome? Do the children there seem happy? How regimented is it? Could you see your child there? Many of our children are super-attuned to the atmosphere of a place so take them along and ask them how it makes them feel.

Research the ethos of the school. Read the rule book, look at how long it is, the tone of it. Education seems to be going through a battle with itself over whether it is about training children military-style in compliance and deference or the sorts of attachment-friendly practices that many of us might recognise as desirable. There are a few schools whose rules and regs defy parody and you'll spot these a mile off. There might be a strong emphasis on what would happen if a child doesn't wear the regulation socks or have a geometry set in their pencil case or greet the teacher in quite the right way. The defence is that children from wayward families are crying out for tight boundaries and thrive within them. There might be some elements of truth in this, but it looks to me suspiciously like some adults are getting off on a massive power trip. Many of our children would not last five minutes in such places. What our children are desperate for are safety and relationships with trusted adults that can last the course because this is what they've missed. Only then can they begin the dangerous business of learning new things. ('What?! You haven't come to school prepared to learn?' 'Listen mate, you're lucky we even made it into school.')

Narrow down your choices and ask for an appointment to visit each school. If you're concerned that your child might find school difficult then my advice is to be open and honest. Tell the staff about your child's status and explain what their difficulties are. Explore how the school would react to situations you might commonly experience, for example, what if your child is late, doesn't have the right equipment, runs out of a lesson, or hasn't slept from the anxiety of something that's happened during the school day? What would their response be?

The absolute key to our child's success at secondary school is in my view communication and teamwork. Will the school consider you as an essential part of the team? Will they drop you a quick email if something has happened at school that day? Are they open to discussions about how best your child could be supported? Are they willing to attend training and read books and guides? The flip side is that we too have to approach our relationship with school openly. We too need to be able to hear difficult things, to work with compromise and to recognise that schools are working under intense pressure.

What is the school's track record of supporting adopted and looked-after children? What support is in place? What's the designated teacher like?

Is there support in place for children who can't manage a full timetable? If a child is removed or removes themselves from a lesson, where do they go? Is there a special classroom or support centre? What are the staff like who work there? What sort of welcome would your child get? If it's anything short of 'Hello, Daniel, it's nice to see you, would you like a drink?' followed by 'Tell me all about it' then it might not be suitable. If it's a sending home with a stern letter, or a week full of detentions then personally I would politely excuse myself and never return.

Do you have another sibling who is at the same school or who will be following on? How well will your siblings manage their relationship if they are in the same school? Will one interfere with the friendships of the other? Does one prefer to stay under the radar and find the attention their sibling draws to them difficult to cope with? These are extra factors that those of us with more than one child have to consider very carefully indeed. My children went to different secondary schools and although I don't have a crystal ball (thank goodness) I'm pretty sure that it made at least one of their school lives significantly less complicated. Despite the logistical problems, it made my life easier as well.

We can do all the groundwork and research we like, but there are still many variables that will determine how well our children do at school or how well school does for our children. There are no failsafe methods of choosing a school and at some point we take a leap of faith and hope for the best. What's certain though is that choosing a school is the easy part.

Transition to big school

No time is ever wasted on preparing our children to go up to big school, especially as the move coincides with the onset of adolescence. Great timing!

Many of our children are pant-wettingly scared at the prospect of going to big school and you will probably have to do your best to hold them emotionally through this transition. Unfortunately it takes place after a VERY LONG summer holiday, which makes the whole thing rather more drawn out and painful than it need be. I'm told it's something to do with having to get the harvest in, which frankly sounds like a poor excuse for the second[1] longest summer of your life. I sometimes wonder how it could be made any more difficult.

It is crucial that your child gets to visit their new school as many times as possible and that they get to spend time with adults who will be supporting them once they start school proper. If they have a need for additional support then really they should get to meet their teaching assistant, their form teacher and the staff who work in the student support centre. They should be made to feel welcome and it is important that staff express how much they are looking forward to your child starting school. Make sure that your child has pictures and names of the staff. These might be available on the school website. One tour of the school is not likely to be enough as our child may spend most of that tour feeling completely overwhelmed and confused. Several tours could take place with a smartphone or a camera to hand so that our child can record their visit and recount it back to us and to the teachers at their existing school. Asking them to talk you through their visit and show you their pictures will give you a good idea what is making them feel anxious and will give you the opportunity to address those anxieties. One of the tours should ideally focus

---

1   The first longest being the frankly horrific summer after final year exams.

on safety. You and I may assume that an establishment such as a school is safe, but our children may not. They will need to know there is a signing-in procedure, they'll need to see the gates and fences and they'll need to understand that all adults working at the school have passed certain checks. They may also need to know about the fire alarm system, the fire drill and all matters safety and security until it drives you bananas. Something that you may also have to tackle is the rumours: the new kids get their heads shoved down the toilets, they get burned with cigarettes, that kind of thing. I can remember being anxious about these stories over an entire summer and I had no level of trauma at all.

Sharing our own experiences of starting a new school can be useful, as long as we're mindful of where our child is at. I favour sharing things like 'I used to worry I would forget how to get to school and get lost on the way.' That way, if it rings true for them, we can talk it through and perhaps walk them to school a few times. It can be a more effective way of hitting on anxieties than facing them head-on with an 'Are you scared of?' question.

All that said, moving up to big school is also an exciting time and we shouldn't forget to share the excitement with them too. Some of being successful during this time is about showing enthusiasm and being up for the adventure. For all its challenges, there are new and exciting opportunities too and given the right introduction and the right support our children could, when they're ready, grasp these and flourish. The message is 'We're all going to help you and it'll be fine.'

Many therapeutic parents report the existence of the 'honeymoon period'. This is the perhaps first four to six weeks at the very start of the first term at the new school. Things can go so swimmingly during the honeymoon period that we allow intense feelings of optimism to creep in and staff at the new school may begin wondering if we were making it all up for attention and due to some form of Munchausen by Proxy. My advice is to take these few weeks as probably very much-needed self-care. You will know whether your child's magnificent coping is in fact the frantic paddling of a little duckling against the current and will suspect that duckling will run out of coping in catastrophic fashion, but still, make the most of this time of relative calm, regroup and recharge.

Supporting our children in school

Supporting our children through secondary school is a team game. It may not be clear from the start who belongs to the team but at its core must be you, their form teacher, year head, the person in charge of additional needs and your child's support person or people, whoever they are. Other team members may identify themselves by being kind and demonstrating they accept and value our child. They might be the maths teacher, the art teacher or the PE teacher. Then there will be an outer circle of nice people who make our child's passage through school smoother and more enjoyable: the person who works on the reception desk, the lab assistant, the caretaker. It might be worthwhile starting to identify who all these people are.

In recent years some great resources[2] provided by some great people have become available that set out practical ways of supporting care-experienced children in school. It is heartening that these sorts of approaches are now becoming mainstream. When I started out it all seemed a bit 'woo woo' and I had to

2   Emma Gore Langton and Katherine Boy, *Becoming an Adoption-Friendly School* (Jessica Kingsley Publishers, 2017); Louise Michelle Bombèr, *What About Me? Inclusive Strategies to Support Pupils with Attachment Difficulties Make it Through the School Day* (Worth Publishing, 2011); 'Welcoming an adopted child to your secondary school', Adoption UK, www.adoptionuk.org.uk.

work hard to come over as a sensible person who hadn't lost her marbles. It's well worth recommending written resources to school and one would hope that these are becoming familiar. There is still no substitute for face-to-face training though. I went to hear Louise Bombèr deliver a day of training to school staff in an out-of-the-way venue. There must have been at least 500 people there. You know when you can tell that a message is hitting the right note and that a great many of those 500 people will go back to their schools with a different way of seeing the children they work with? That's what happened. No matter how hard we try to how skilled we are at delivering the message, it's far more powerful when it's delivered by a great and experienced speaker and backed by a well-known charity or a local authority. My advice is to encourage not only those working directly with your child, but school leaders as well, to go to this kind of training. It could reap huge rewards for many children.

I'm not going to go into all the ways that schools can support our children because many have set that out better than I could, but what I will do is focus on those aspects of support that I think are the most important and the role that we can play as a crucial part of the team.

Timetable
Have a copy of the lesson timetable displayed somewhere accessible but perhaps not in-your-face and unavoidable (school-phobics may not appreciate that). Expect it to be destroyed/lost/defaced. Keep a second copy in a safe place.

School bag
When we think 'younger child' it can help us to see when we need to step in and make sure our child has the right books and equipment for the day. Some of our children may take against

us going anywhere near their bags. If this is the case, perhaps check after bedtime, remove the mouldy sandwiches and add in what's missing.

Spare kit

For the chaotic, be sure to have plenty of spare stationery, lunch hardware, uniform and PE kit. It's not so easy with expensive rugby shorts and suchlike on the kit list but you may be able to get your hands on some hand-me-downs. It stands to reason that we have to label absolutely everything and that we'll probably get to be on first name terms with the person who manages lost property. It's good for teachers and parents to practise the art of acceptance when it comes to kit. No amount of nagging or punishment is likely to influence organisational difficulties, in fact, they may even make the situation worse.

School Mum or Dad

Many of our children's difficulties with school can be eased if they have a School Mum or a School Dad. The proper name for a School Mum or Dad is an Attachment Figure: the person or group of people who perform a similar role to you but at school. This person has to be someone they like, or who they can grow to like and form an attachment with. School Mum or Dad looks out for them, takes them out of a lesson well before they tell the teacher to f**k off, notices when they are sad or angry, is pleased to see them, knows how to help regulate them and understands attachment and early life trauma and the playful, accepting, curious and empathic approaches that can be so effective in connecting with our children. It's a really difficult job and I would say needs lots of back-up and probably more than one School Mum or Dad. School Mum or Dad is a good person to be the main contact with home.

Don't sweat the small stuff

If you are anything like me then nothing is likely to render you more stony-faced and ready for a fight at the end of the school day than a phone call or email detailing every one of our child's misdemeanours that lands just before they arrive home. Our poor child bounds in through the door hoping for a welcome and a couple of biscuits and we hit them with a barrage of our own shame and dysregulation.

During the school week there may be lots of mini- and not so mini-dramas. One of the benefits of a team around our child is that we can agree with that team that they will let us know the significant stuff (in a non-shaming and constructive way) and hold on to the rest.

We will all, parents, carers and school staff, have to hone our 'don't sweat the small stuff' skills as our child progresses through senior school. I've said this before, but it's worth repeating: most of what we consider to be big stuff, is small stuff – forgetting to bring in a pen, being a few minutes late for a lesson, refusing to wear a school coat, not being able to sit through assembly, taking ages to change for PE – these are annoying, sure, but they are small stuff. If we raise the temperature in reaction to every piece of small stuff, we run out of headroom for the big stuff. School Mum or Dad may have to do a considerable amount of mopping up of small stuff.

After-school dysregulation

We all know the drill, don't we? Our child is doing well at school, or is at least not getting into trouble, being quiet, ducking below the radar and yet they come home and spill dysregulated trauma all over the house and everyone in it. Because it happens at home, it must be down to something at home, in other words, our terrible parenting. Here's the thing. Trauma is like a big balloon;

apply pressure at one end by squeezing it and it expands at the other end. The amount of trauma is the same, it just moves. In order to reduce the overall amount of trauma, we must work as a team, home and school, together, in a joined-up way. If our child is falling in through the door at the end of the day, screaming at us and smashing things up, then that is everyone's business and everyone must explore the reasons why and the measures that will be taken to reduce the total pressure on the child.

As the parent who anxiously waits at home for the nuclear missile to hit, what can we do to try to defuse the situation? Firstly, I think most of the useful work is done in calm times and in conversation with our child: 'That moment when you arrive home is dangerous for us, it's when you're a bit skitty and I get annoyed and we fall out. Does that make sense? How can we avoid it?' 'I completely understand why you get home feeling skitty, it's because the school day is tough and you have to let it all out.'

Options that you might want to explore are whereabouts you are in the house when your child comes in. Is it better if you are immediately there, or busying yourself nearby? Are things easier if you leave a drink and some food out that they can grab? Do they need permission to run up to their room to cool down before they speak to you? Is it better if you are not even in the house, or would that lead to worse trouble? Is there a sibling coming in from school as well who could be in the firing line? My experience is that being right there and, worse still, immediately asking how the day went does not make for happy times. I learned to make myself physically busy during times I thought might get testy. This helped to keep my own anxiety down and avoid eye contact whilst maintaining a presence. Of course it didn't always work and the return home could be very explosive and challenging indeed and that's when we had to look at reducing the stresses at school. If you are experiencing aggressive behaviours on the return home from school then keep a written record of events and seek help. This is covered in greater depth in the section 'Aggressive and violent behaviours' in Chapter 9. I presuppose that you or your partner is in the house for the big return but you may not be. You may have good reasons to be out of the home at 4 o'clock like, say, a job and your child may return to an empty house and they may regulate themselves or they may not and you may miss out on the dysregulation and it might get saved up for your return later in the day. It seems to be something that catches up with us one way or another.

If our children bounce in wanting to tell us all about their day, listening with curiosity and without judgement can be difficult too. They may want to tell us what a cow Mrs Whoever is and how unfairly she dealt with a situation. You may have a fair idea whether Mrs Whoever is a cow or whether she has faced a wave of difficult behaviour. You may have to show empathy in a hedging your bets kind of way, but if Mrs Whoever really is a cow then I think it's all right to fully empathise and to explore what is unfair about her approach to her students. Remaining on the side of another adult who is clearly behaving unfairly can, I think, be damaging to our relationship with our child, who after all is working hard at learning to trust us. It may be possible to do some useful exploration around what motivates people to behave in certain ways. This may be enough to enable our children to contain themselves in those lessons, or the team around our child may have to look into changing that class. In my experience one poor teacher can significantly destabilise the relationally challenged child. Everyone will know that teacher is poor and certainly all the other children will. Whilst they may be skilled at putting up and shutting up, our child will be the one who lacks the skills and regulation to avoid getting into trouble. One can argue that they need to learn to keep their mouths shut, but at what cost? Adults around traumatised children need to be mindful that they are not setting them up to fail and that sometimes means making brave and unusual decisions.

Reduced timetable

As I mentioned, we are not aiming to set our children up to fail. Carrying around vast amounts of anxiety and feeling unsafe means that our kids are draining their batteries much more quickly than their peers and may not be able to manage a full timetable or a full suite of exam subjects.

End-of-school exams could not fall at a worse time for many of our most traumatised young people who can start unravelling quite catastrophically at this point. It really is not worth insisting they plough on with a full set of subjects if there is a high risk they are going to fail the lot. This is a time in their lives when they need to experience some success. I realise that many schools will baulk at this. Perhaps there's a worry that if one child is offered a reduced timetable there will be a flood of requests for the same. I don't know about that and in my simplistic mind that shouldn't be a barrier to doing right by our children who have so much stacked against them.

Homework and revision

If your child finds it impossible to do their homework at home then I can only say that I know how difficult it is to get this across to school without coming over all 'flaky parent'. It seems like an easy thing for them to do, half an hour of maths, some geography questions, doesn't it? Everyone else can manage it, so why can't they? It could be a matter of how far we are willing to push it.

Who doesn't look forward to an entire weekend ruined by homework: a door kicked in, a screen smashed, a family left ragged and weakened? Families like ours cannot afford for our relationships to be put under strain by homework. Maintaining relationships, particularly through the teen years, is difficult enough, and it's crucial if we are to help our children navigate their way through these most destabilising of times. Is it worth throwing our relationship with our child under the bus for the sake of homework? The answer has to be a great big 'no'.

If school and homework pressures threaten to rock your family then my advice is to get that timetable reduced and set aside the time that is freed up during the school day to get any homework done, alongside a trusted adult. Our children need school and home to be separate; they don't benefit from the stresses and strains of school being imported into their home life. For their progress and healing to be maintained, home must remain a place of safety, calm and enjoyment. That goes for us too. It's difficult enough being the parent of a relationally damaged, dysregulated child without being the homework enforcer as well. The two roles are entirely incompatible.

Curriculum trigger points

One of the important roles of the team round our child is to be cognisant of parts of the curriculum that may be particularly difficult and sensitive. I recommend having a particularly close look at the PSHE (Personal, Social and Health Education) curriculum as there can be some landmines in place waiting to explode all over your family. Drugs, alcoholism, abortion, domestic abuse, animal cruelty might all be subjects that carry a weight of meaning and pain and exploring these in a class of 30 other children may be unbearable. We had a particularly harrowing evening following a lesson on child abuse. Terrible memories and fears were dragged to the surface without a safe adult to help regulate. Teachers of PHSE would be advised to be mindful that some of the subjects they cover are about the real life of some of their students and the fallout may occur outside of school, perhaps somewhere that isn't safe for that fallout to take place. Displaying and talking about drugs paraphernalia may also be another highly sensitive trigger for some children. Again, these are risks that real children are exposed to in real life, not in theory.

Parents' evening

If there's one event that brings me to the verge of emotional crumbling it's attending parents' evening with a shame-ridden child. It's hellish. If it's hellish for you and your child too then you can do what I did and refuse to put yourselves through it. All the relevant feedback you need could be provided by the team round the child, in a supportive way. If, on the other hand, your child performs well at school and the event is celebratory, then be my guest. And if you particularly enjoy being eyeballed by angry parents and lectured at by disapproving teachers then also, be my guest.

Reports

Your child's support team may or may not be able to influence the way reports are worded and the tone they take. Some of ours didn't make it home, others came home in tiny pieces of shame to be assembled like an horrific end-of-term jigsaw. Repetitive comments like 'X needs to learn to pay attention or he will never learn anything' drive me nuts. Either get them worded constructively, or have them sent in the post. And while I'm at it, for every negative, blaming comment, there should be a corresponding action. How are we going to support this child to do better?

One of the risks of reading a negatively worded report is that we get muscled up for a fight with our child the moment they walk in through the door. If you've been emotionally hijacked by a report, my advice is to sleep on it; don't get bounced into a big, messy fallout.

When our children have a strong team of supportive, attuned adults around them, who get what they are about and how they've become the child they see before them, school can be a positive and rewarding experience. We made a big change to get to the right school for one of our children and it paid off. It wasn't perfect, because these things never are, but the professionalism and care with which we were treated was exceptional and it kept us afloat when nothing else was on offer. For a few years it was the best support I had as well. This was achieved in a mainstream school, with all of the stresses and strains that mainstream schools have to cope with. There were a few individuals who made a great difference, but the temperature was set by the school as a whole from the leadership team to the office staff. It was a caring and nurturing place.

Exams

One of the biggest psychological challenges I have faced is coming to terms with what the measures of success are. What constitutes a successful time at school? In another life I would have been a big supporter of all things educational for my children. I believe in the transformative powers of education and I've benefited from a (reasonably) good education myself. However, the big lesson for me has been that relationships and acceptance sit at the root of a relationally traumatised child and young person's development and until these are secure, no amount of teaching will bypass them. Once I got my head around the acceptance part of that, I did a lot better. I had to do a lot of thinking about the imagined fistful of exam passes and who exactly they were for. I know there are many routes to a successful life and that young people more often than not find their own way, using their own skills and talents. It was only when I finally felt that in my bones that my support became genuine and unconditional. That's not to say we don't remain ambitious for our children, but it's ambitious tailored to them.

A measure of success might be a few exams with decent grades, it might be what's required to access a college course or to go on and study subjects at a higher level, or success may be remaining in education and making it to the end and that's a fine ambition to have as well.

Exam time looms on the horizon like a period of bad weather and maybe the best we can do is get lots of nice food in and batten down the hatches. Leading up to exam time it's worth cancelling anything extraneous that will cause extra pressure on top of the already humungous pressure and make life as easy for everyone as possible. This might be about how to get through it, rather than how to do it well. On top of exams, which come on top of everything else, there may also be what will possibly be the most seismic transition our child has had to negotiate: the transition from school to whatever comes next. Great!

During exam time I learned that no amount of nagging resulted in any revision being done. I didn't need to learn that any offer of help would be seen as a threat and must be fought off at all costs. I know that in some families, parents or older siblings are able to help with revision timetables and topics and so on and if that's possible it's to be celebrated, but if yours isn't one of those families then here's my advice:

Make sure that appropriate measures are in place to maximise your child's chances of success. Do they need extra time? Do they work better in a small room away from the main exam room? Do they require a scribe? If your child has a School Mum or Dad then they will need to be fully present during exam time, offering calm consistency and encouragement.

Remove yourself emotionally and psychologically from the pressure of the exams and the expectation of results.

Provide stability and routine, good food and a calm presence until you are dizzy with it.

If your child does zero revision, try to be as OK with that as you can be. It might be worth expressing, one or two times, your concern that zero revision might not lead to the result your child is hoping for, then leave it at that.

Get in as much self-care as is humanly possible. You have a long summer ahead, punctuated by results day. It may feel like the longest summer of your life, and not in a 'hooray, I'm going to travel around Europe' kind of a way.

Mentally prepare yourself for a refusal to go into school on an exam day. If you think you'll be able to entice them in then think through your strategy, if not then be prepared for the consequences of that to play out. If your child reacts badly to pressure and panic, then you need to picture yourself not adding to the pressure and panic. Think of yourself as the safe port in the exam storm.

Provide comforting food. There's nothing quite like a surprise, unconditional tube of Pringles and a share-size bag of Wispa bites to help a person feel a little bit better and I speak with some experience here.

If exam time is teeth-grindingly awful in your house, then step outside, smell the summer air and remind yourself it will soon be over.

Approaching results day with zero expectation is advisable. I also recommend getting your head straight beforehand with regards to your reactions to certain possible results and the saint-like amount of acceptance you are going to deliver. With a bit of luck, you may not need all of this, but I did, loads of it. As it happens I'm quite proud of how we managed results day. 'Well done for getting to the end of school' was our message, 'we're proud of you.' We may also have had a conversation about how the education system is weighted heavily against children who are carrying a big load of trauma on their backs. It's when the chips are down and our child is expecting us to breathe fire that we can make our truest and strongest gestures of love and solidarity. It's worth getting this one right.

Further education

Where I live, the brightest children get to stay on in the comforting arms of school and continue their studies, while the less academically able get to go to a large, scary college a bus ride or two from home where they most likely don't know anyone and where they will enjoy a less than packed timetable and bucketloads of spare time they can spend with all the other dysregulated kids. It's an interesting way of doing things. Amongst our children, the odds certainly seem stacked in favour of the academically able.

Leaving their school at 16 may be something our loved ones have hankered after for a long time but no matter how much they enjoyed or didn't enjoy school, leaving it is a big deal. We may need to employ some of our old measures like suggesting they go back and visit and asking if School Mum or School Dad would drop them the occasional email.

If leaving school at 16 is a massive deal, then starting college is mega-massive and I think the gravity of that change is under-estimated. Unlike school, the support around young people at college is, how can I put this, flimsy. You may find yourself having to do an awful lot of legwork to get your child's difficulties recognised and catered for and you may struggle to even find someone willing to talk to you. And the emphasis at college is being treated and behaving more like an adult, taking responsibility, being self-motivated and organised. A huge step up in expectation alongside a huge drop in support right at the point many of our children are at peak adolescence. What could possibly go wrong? Try asking School Mum or Dad to go into college and do a kind of information exchange and handover and provide college with relevant resources. You may just find someone who is willing and able to go on this next stage of the educational journey with you.

At this point in our child's education, it may not be viable for you to continue to advocate at all. Those with issues around control and a need to appear invincible around their new peers may make it impossible for you to have any sway at all. This may be the time when our young people push hard up against boundaries and consequences in real, high-definition terms and work hard to keep us distanced from their new life. Their success at college may depend on how much unresolved trauma they are carrying, their abilities to self-regulate and the peer group they fall into. We may have to work very hard indeed just to remain connected. Another important consideration is whether we have a younger child whose needs have been in the background all this time.

I don't mean to sound beaten and I know that many of our young people go on to find success and a new lease of life at college. The freedom from having to study subjects you didn't like or couldn't grasp and the opportunity to follow something you've chosen can be truly liberating. It might be the first time our loved ones have really experienced being talented at something. What a great feeling! If this is your child's experience then it really is something wonderful to behold. If it isn't, then hang on in there and keep reading.

Apprenticeships and work

For those who just can't do classrooms and hard learning, who are much better at learning through doing and who get along much better with a group of sensible, regulated adults than they do with their less sensible, less well-regulated peers, an apprenticeship or job can be the answer that unlocks a whole seam of potential. For those who can't do those things but who haven't yet mastered the art of turning up on time, doing what they're told and accepting some supervision the world of work can be a great shock. Real-world consequences are very much alive in the real world.

The great thing about apprenticeships is that you can start at the bottom and work your way up, in a semi-protected environment, while maturity sets in. There is, however, a great difference in the quality of apprenticeships on offer. Some offer good training and supervision, with perhaps some time spent at college whereas others, well, not so much. This is not the place to moan about those employers playing the system, so all I'll say is beware. We may have to steer our loved ones towards the former, although they may doggedly resist our steerage and we may have to watch on and witness a few false starts.

Employment is a whole other kettle of fish, especially for those with few qualifications and not much work/life experience. Low hourly rates and zero hour contracts may just suit for a while but the lack of routine and constant change of working hours and the possible rejection felt when the desired shifts aren't offered may be a bridge too far.

As much as we may wish that our loved ones could plan a path to the future, see the stepping stones required to reach a goal and perhaps accept less money now, in the hope of more in the future, some simply do not yet have those cognitive skills. The teenage brain in general is not brilliant at planning steps towards an end goal and with the added layer of trauma, our kids may be severely hampered in that respect. When you absolutely live in the now and cannot risk putting aside something of the now, for a future possible reward, planning a career path is something they may just not be able to manage yet. On top of that, they may not appreciate how difficult it is to live on the minimum wage. £250 is loads, isn't it? It might take years of doing sh**ty jobs before the pennies drop.

It's easy enough for me to write all this, but feeling the shock waves of another lost job, witnessing the chaos and the fallout, the shame and the anger is of course extremely testing for parents who have always hoped for the best for our children and who know their talents and potential. The adult world catches up way before many are ready and, try as we might, our ability to guide, warn and support can be hampered by a developmentally unready young person, who finds it difficult to accept that we might be right. Learning the hard way was never more relevant and often all we can do is be there to sympathise when the latest amazing opportunity hasn't quite turned out as expected.

CHAPTER 8

Siblings

If you are therapeutically parenting siblings, here are some of the things you might witness in your home. If you can tick off more than a couple, then I wouldn't mind betting you're in need of a sit-down and a head massage.

Supervision. You can't leave your children alone in the house together, or even in the same room. Other people, innocent people, will express disbelief and even suspect that you are behaving over-protectively or even hysterically. They don't appreciate that if you left your children alone together there is a moderate chance they would kill each other or the house would get burnt down.

When they were toddlers you fantasised about a time when they would be mature enough to have a healthy enough relationship that you could go out for the odd hour now and then and do something just for you, maybe even get a job. That time just keeps moving further and further out of sight.

Dysregulation. On the rare occasions that your children choose to spend time together, things soon become excitable, boisterous and 'over the top'. It's like they don't know how to be together and the sheer novelty along with the lack of skills is too much of a challenge. There may be signs that they both really want this thing to work, but they just can't and the disappointment may be tremendous. It's sad that trauma gets in the way of so many good things, and healthy sibling relationships may be one of those casualties.

Sabotage. One of your children likes going out and doing interesting things. The other may like doing the same interesting things, but wouldn't dare admit it because they would rather their brother or sister suffer than everyone have a nice time out together. They will do everything in their power, including refusing to get out of bed and spreading themselves across the entire back seat of the car in order to ensure the trip out is impossible. And because you can't leave them alone on their own unsupervised, either no one can go out, or you take the willing child out while your partner stays at home. That's if you even have a partner. You may start to forget what spending time with your partner, or indeed any functional adult who isn't paid to spend time with you, feels like.

In-y and Out-y. One has an 'out-y' trauma style and the other has an 'in-y' trauma style. Out-y is loud, sometimes behaves aggressively, is dysregulated and 'attention-seeking' but can explore difficult things when the time is right. In-y is quiet, 'happy', a 'crowd-pleaser' and will do anything to avoid talking about difficult things. They require subtly different types of parenting. Out-y is on and in your mind all of the time. In-y is 'fine' and drifts off the radar, despite you knowing they're not really fine. Attempts to move in-y centre stage causes out-y to escalate to the point you cannot help but put their needs first.

You feel guilty most of the time that neither child is really getting what they need from you, that you are being pushed hither and thither by their traumatised ways of doing relationships.

It's an ambush. Jealousy is everywhere, particularly when one has been recognised at school for doing something great, becomes engaged in a new hobby or has a birthday. It feels too dangerous for your brother or sister to soak up all the attention and so it's time to ambush their glory.

A friend of yours is a friend of mine. One child cannot help but interfere in the friendships of the other, at school, online, anywhere they can. They try to humiliate them, or pile into dramas. They find it difficult to make friends of their own and they can't bear for their brother or sister to have any either. If a friend comes home after school, the sibling will be right there. 'Leave us alone!' Not flipping likely.

What's yours is mine. They steal from each other, or at least you think they do. One becomes incensed that something has been taken. Retribution is sought and then reciprocated. It's serve and return but not the good kind the books talk about. Nothing of any value is safe in the house. It is possible though that the original offence didn't actually take place. It's impossible to tell, especially once you have lost all logical powers of deduction.

More than sibling rivalry. One is intimidating and abusive towards the other. Much of it happens in secret. One day you witness an incident out of the corner of your eye and you can't believe it. The victim tells you that it's been going on for ages and that they've been trying to tell you about it. You feel terribly guilty and full of worry. You try to pick apart what's going on and explain that that kind of behaviour is not acceptable. The perpetrator will go through a cycle of denial, blame, victimhood and anger and you will get nowhere. The victim will say, 'It's OK, Mum, I'm used to it.' The guilt washes over you again. You wonder if the conditions in their birth family home are being replicated in yours.

Tit-for-tat. One child plays a practical joke on the other. It's not funny and you think it's probably abusive. It might be they poured water on to their sibling's mattress or switched on their bedroom light in the middle of the night. The victim gets them back by carrying out something similar. The tit-for-tat escalates to a point where your family life feels like a Lord of the Flies re-enactment. It takes an awful lot of your energy and quick thinking to put an end to it.

Ganging up. When the chips are really down and both siblings feel aggrieved at something you either have or haven't done, which you promised on your life you would do, or something like that, they will gang up against you. It will be like nothing you have ever read about or been told about. You may find yourself having to be über-strong in order to overcome the might of the combined trauma. They are of course scared that you may not be strong enough. It's the ultimate test. If we falter, things get turned up a notch.

Threat detection. One sibling is cautious and has a finely tuned threat detector whilst the other is attracted by threat like a moth to a flame and acts like a lightning rod mainlining risk into your family life. Their ways of keeping themselves safe are not only polar opposite but incompatible. The dynamic is complicated and it becomes difficult if not impossible to keep them both safe.

Who's the parent around here? When one of the first lessons children learn is that adults and, in particular parents are not to be trusted and you, an adult and a parent, arrive on the scene, even with all your good intentions, you are already on a sticky wicket. Eldest child may battle you for parental control, their younger siblings may both prefer their 'parenting' and detest it in equal measure. It's another test of our staying power and our resilience. 'I am your parent and you can trust me and it is safe for all of you to trust me' we demonstrate over and over. This web of brain-dissolving complicatedness is known as 'the trauma bond'. I suspect there's a lot more to be uncovered about the trauma bond.

The thing is, when we share our lives with more than one child who has experienced neglect, abuse and loss in their early lives, we become the source of safety and the means by which their needs can be met. Seen through the lens of trauma, our capacity, even if it could be trusted to hold up, is dangerously limited: there simply isn't enough of us to go around. Therefore our ability to care, our attention, our love must be fought over, doubted, sabotaged. It's a matter of survival and no amount of reasoning and reassuring can overcome that most basic of human instincts. This is another endurance test during which we must prove ourselves.

There are many uncomfortable and awkward truths about early life trauma and permanence and one of the most significant of those is siblings. Everything that is good and well-intentioned says that keeping siblings together is the right thing to do. And if you parent care-experienced siblings, your experience may be just that. If your experience is of something far more complicated then I suspect you fall within the majority. My own view is that it's fine for the state to set the expectation and the preference for siblings to be kept together, but without adequate research on the outcomes for children and more importantly adequate support for those of us tearing ourselves apart trying to parent more than one related child at the same time, the state ought to be a bit more circumspect. It should also be more mindful that cute but traumatised toddlers grow up to be less cute, traumatised teenagers. That's when things can get much more tricky. If parenting one teenager who has experienced profound early life trauma is difficult, parenting two or more can be a feat of incredible human endurance. I've spoken to many therapeutic parents who report that despite great moments, it's been one long exercise in damage limitation. That's pretty much where I stand and I very much wish it wasn't. This isn't something, you'll understand, that I post on social media or generally go shouting about.

I've got into some hot water for my views on this matter. My views, as it happens, are built on years of wrestling to meet everyone's needs and the dawning realisation of the impossibility of this. That's not to say that Mr D and I have done a terrible job, because I don't think we have, but there have been winners and losers. I believe that the drive to keep siblings together must not overtake an individual child's need to be cared for appropriately and safely, albeit with relationships preserved that can be tailored to suit needs and that can wax and wane over time, as circumstances and wishes change.

None of this is any help if we are parenting siblings right now and struggling to manage their differing, clashing needs, so here goes.

This stuff is really difficult

Ever spend time in someone else's house and witness their children rubbing along, having the odd disagreement, recovering, perhaps even enjoying each other's company? If you're anything like me then glimpses like this can be a revelation. This is what family life is like, for most families. Isn't it lovely? Isn't it peaceful? Doesn't it feel safe? Don't you ache for your family life to be like this? Of course families have many, hidden currents, but I've never experienced anything like the sibling difficulties I know, in anyone else's home, other than in those of my therapeutic parent friends.

We live on the front line of the dirtiest, most uncompromising battlefield there is: the battle for human survival. It is psychologically, emotionally and even physically demanding. I point this out because it's important to acknowledge how very hard it is living with traumatised children who are fighting with each other for their lives. If you are buckling under the strain, then give yourself a break. You are doing something amazing for your children, even if they don't yet realise it. Keeping siblings together isn't the fairytale it's often made out to be, so it's likely that even the professionals around you don't really get the degree of sibling rivalry you're trying to referee. Allow yourself a heap of regular self-care and self-compassion.

Divide and conquer

An obvious way of calming troubled waters if you have a partner is to regularly split your children by sharing them out and taking them out separately. It's more than possible that both will benefit from some quality one-to-one time and we may benefit in being reminded of the person our child is when their sibling weaponry is offline. There may be some jealousies to negotiate and for that reason it might be best to present a fait accompli ('You're coming out with me, your sister is going out with Dad' type of thing). If both favour one parent then there may be some tussling, but I don't need to tell you that. (If you experience inconvenient levels of parent preference then it can be worth establishing opportunities for better bonding with the out-of-favour parent. That unfortunate parent may need to go the extra mile to do something the child really loves doing that the other parent doesn't do with them, so it becomes a special thing. For example, a trip to a meat-based fast food outlet is quite near the top of my 'Places I Would Only Go Under Duress' list, but is something my partner enjoys doing. This makes him popular as long as he's prepared to shell out for some fried chicken.)

Do what works
Figure out which trips work en famille and stick to them. Ours revolve around food and the cinema. We eat out quite a lot and we see a lot of films. We've worked out cheap ways of doing these activities and as we'll never, ever go to Disneyworld or on a safari we reckon this frees up the entertainment budget. Drama-free, good times are bonding and give everyone positive memories to fall back on when the chips (and the fried chicken) are down.

Encourage different interests
Our children need to develop their own personalities with their own likes, dislikes and interests, away from the crushing strain of shared trauma. Where there are opportunities to pursue an interest, or to take part in something like sports, children can develop and grow out of the confines of the home environment and their prescribed role within it. Overwhelming trauma may preclude the development of interests in one or both children and may cause some inter-sibling jealousy. One sibling may really need the other to be contained at home and not to be developing and growing away. If this is causing problems I favour the 'say what you see' approach, at the right time. 'I've noticed that you find it difficult when your brother goes out to play football', 'Perhaps it makes you wish you could do something as part of a team too', 'You're good at different things, perhaps there is something you'd like to do after school?' Conversations like this don't necessarily bring about a sudden desire to join the hockey club, but over time they do help our children to know we have

seen and understood them, and that we still love them the same whether they have outside interests or not.

Separate schools
It came as a gradual shock to me and a gradual shock to my logistical budget that our children were both going to be much better off attending different senior schools. It made life complicated in some practical aspects and less complicated in many other aspects. What happened at school could stay at school, without events being dredged over at home; peer relationships could play out without being interfered with (more or less); and, to put it rather bluntly, one child didn't get saddled with the exploits and notoriety of the other.

Low-key celebrating
I'm guessing you know how this goes. One child gets recognised for an achievement, at school perhaps. We may feel like instantly shouting out, 'That's fantastic! Well done!' as goodness knows, a bit of success greases the wheels of therapeutic parenting, but even a good thing may have to be approached with thought and a bit of planning. If success threatens to rock the boat of family unity then it may be better to mark the achievement in a low-key family way but in a louder more congratulatory way in private with the successful child. If we avoid marking the achievement altogether then trauma wins the day. That's not to say we rub trauma's nose in it.

As is so often the case, it may be beneficial to name the difficulties presented by the achievement, for everyone's benefit: 'We're all pleased for X that he has won the cup, well done, X, and we know this might be difficult for you because you'd like to be celebrated too.' This may be met with denials but that doesn't mean it hasn't hit the spot. We may need to make a point of marking Child Y's achievements sometime soon, even if those achievements aren't about winning cups, trophies and awards.

Happy birthday!

There's nothing like a slice of trauma-informed sibling rivalry to ensure a birthday goes off like a dry box of fireworks. If your siblings can remember each and every birthday their brother or sister ruined then it may be time to get it all out into the open.

'We know you struggle when it's your sister's birthday because you feel like all the attention is on her and you're forgotten.' Depending on how the land lies you could try the 'we're all going to show that we haven't forgotten you' approach. That wins you Star of the Week for full-on empathy and acceptance. Other approaches may involve giving unbirthday child the option to do something else rather than go to their sibling's party or talking to them about how the day can be made easier for them and perhaps giving them an unbirthday present. They may like to be given a special responsibility such as lighting the candles and bringing in the birthday cake. At the end of the day though, everyone deserves a birthday and sometimes our kids just have to like it or lump it and we have to manage the day as best we can whilst building in plenty of recovery time afterwards.

Violence and intimidation

One of the most difficult aspects of sibling relationships to manage is when one or both are aggressive or intimidating towards the other. From my extensive research,[1] it seems most common that one sibling dishes out aggression in the direction of the other, who sometimes responds, but mostly sucks it up. It can become a relationship based on power, control and fear. It's not what we ever expected family life to be like.

---

1   Hours spent in coffee shops with the exhausted parents of warring siblings

In this situation, preventing our children from being harmed by each other has to be our priority. Keeping them apart using Close Supervision is the about the only way we can hope to achieve this, with at least some degree of success, but constant Close Supervision is exhausting and let's face it, not that straightforward with teenagers. Our sensors are set to the 'on' position most of the time and our ears are tuned in to the tell-tale signs that something is about to break out.

Close Supervision is preventative and there's a lot to be said for preventative techniques; however, we cannot be present 24/7 and we cannot carry the responsibility if one child is violent towards the other. It may even take place despite and because of our careful measures. Violence between siblings takes us right to the point where we need to put our stakes in the ground. What is and isn't acceptable in our homes? What constitutes 'normal' sibling rivalry, and at what point are sibling battles abusive and unsafe? These are questions that have clear answers when we're not living in the thick of it. When we are, it's surprising how our judgement can become clouded.

I've had to revisit my own stakes in the ground many times. Sometimes I had to accept that things in our house were more boisterous than in other people's. On occasion I had to take time out and really think about what life must be like for the child on the receiving end and what our family life was showing them about the acceptability of violence in the home, behind closed doors. There was a point when I knew that the line was being crossed, had been for some time. I'd been playing the avoidance game and not taking sides for the sake of family peace, but avoidance when it comes to violence is not, in my experience, a good idea. In a later chapter, 'The Hard Stuff', I cover what I've learned about 'outing' and airing violence but when it comes to violence from one sibling towards another, I learned that sitting on the fence, an approach which had worked to some degree during the early years of sibling rivalry, had begun to look like collusion.

All this is easy to say, but when we realise that things have gone too far, what do we do other than sink into a pool filled with our own guilt and catastrophising? This was my approach. It wasn't a 'one time only' approach – I've been round this particular wheel a few times.

Remind myself that I am the adult and that the only way a sense of order will be re-established is if I re-establish it.

Ditch the guilt. Most people don't live these extremes. I'm doing my best and this is a work-in-progress.

Take whatever time out of the mayhem is possible, even a walk can be enough, or a coffee somewhere. It was important for me to physically remove myself from the house and the psychological soup.

Think about when the violence is happening and why. Think about whether it's taking place at particular times of the day or in particular parts of the house.

Keep a written record.

Revisit resources: books, YouTube videos, even if you've seen them before. It's surprising how something can click into place that didn't seem relevant before.

Talk to other people, peers in the same situation and professionals. Treat it like joint problem-solving. If you sense blame, you might not be talking to the right person. Or the advice might be good but difficult to hear in our worn-down state. Be prepared to hear challenging advice and to make changes. Living with violence can make us react very defensively.

When I think I've got a good handle on what's going on and I feel a bit stronger, I consider holding a family conference. I announce that this is what will happen and ask for everyone's input beforehand. If one particular sibling is on the receiving end of the violence, it's important that their views and experiences are heard. They might be more comfortable writing something down. Other members of the family may need to express how fed up they are living with the constant battles. The conference itself will have to be run carefully in order that it doesn't set off an immediate shame response. Even if it isn't appropriate to hold a family conference, the messages and the approach are still the way to go in my experience.

Holding a family meeting

Decide where and when, perhaps around the table, after a meal. Snacks can act as an encouragement and an icebreaker. Decide on the rules of the conference, such as 'no one is going to be mean to anyone or blame anyone' and 'we're not going to get into the detail of any particular incident' and 'once the conference is over, we're going to draw a line and start afresh'.

Setting the scene

'We're all miserable, we want life to be better for all of us, because we deserve it.'

'We want to help all of us to get along better.'

'I care about you and that's why I want to sort this out.'

'It's just not on that there are members of this family that don't feel safe/get hurt.'

'It is never acceptable for one member of the family to hit another.'

'It is never acceptable for a boy/large boy/almost adult male to hit a girl.'

I realise I'm wandering on to dangerous ground here, but I'm sure you get that I know that girls dish out violence on boys too. Either way, one day our daughters (and our sons) will grow up and have partners and, my goodness, we don't want them choosing the violent ones, out of some sense of searching out the familiar. If there's anything we can do to prevent this, I believe that's getting it out in the open, talking about what we have a right to expect from others and about power, control and self-worth. My dearest child, you should never have to experience violence, emotional abuse or control from anyone, especially not a partner.

Joint problem-solving

'The risky time is when you both get home from school. How can it be organised so there are no clashes?'

'We're going to agree who uses the bathroom and when.'

'The most fights are over the Xbox, how can we reduce that stress?'

'He gets angry when he's trying to sleep and you are talking loudly on Skype. Let's agree the times when Skyping can happen.'

Set out the agreement

'You do not go into each other's bedrooms.'

'If there is a disagreement you come to me and we'll sort it out together.'

'I'll leave food and a drink out for you for when you get home from school, take it to your room and I'll look in on you after half an hour.'

And because there may be measures we can take to reduce the stresses of home life, 'We're going to get you an Xbox each so you no longer have to fight over one.' (Sharing skills may be a great ambition in other families, but insisting on it in ours can be a fool's errand. My advice is to avoid the need to share where you possibly can.)

Hear the complaints

There are likely to be complaints, of course there are. Many of our children long ago came to the conclusion that in order to get their needs met they had to take control and the family conference, the planting of the stake into the ground is the way we demonstrate we are regaining control during a time of chaos. That's not to say we are making a land grab for control. Success in these situations is usually about our children retaining a reasonable level of control. If they think we're taking it all, they may well just fight harder.

'When I tell you about something you never sort it out/you never believe me.' 'So you don't trust me to sort it out, so you do it yourself? I'm going to try harder to show you I'm taking you seriously and acting fairly. You might not always like my response so we're going to have to work at that.'

'He'll just go into my room anyway.' 'We're all going to have to keep to what we've agreed, all of us, it's important. What do you think, X? Are you going to be able to keep out of her room? What will help you to do this?'

'Yesterday he did <such and such described in great detail> *and he's just a* <somethingorother> *and you are a* <somethingevenworse>.' *This may be an attempt to drive you into the detail in order to regain control. Take extra care not to get suckered in and remind everyone of the rules you set out at the start of the conference.*

Stern warning and reconciliation

In our house, if the stern warning comes first, there is a high chance of a sudden reaction and a refusal to take any part in the process, or an argumentative and blocking stance being taken. For that reason I put the stern warning near the end. Your experience may of course be very different. The stern warning might go something like this:

'You've both done well to take part in this, to help make our lives better. You need to know that if someone gets hurt or frightened, it's really not OK. It's not OK to hurt someone and then ask for a tenner and go out with your friends, it's not OK to hurt someone, then demand the wifi goes on for longer, or you get a lift somewhere. And I don't enjoy saying this, but if someone gets badly hurt in our house, I will call the police. If it happened on the street, it would be against the law and the attacker would be arrested. It's no different here.'

This last bit is not, I would suggest, something you say frequently and certainly not unless you are living with a real threat of physical hurt. I don't agree with reminding our children they could 'end up in jail' for things like stealing or whatever because I think it just reaffirms their view that they are bad, terrible people and I suspect that it just drives behaviours until we either do or do not call the police. If we don't then our power amounts to nothing but empty threats and if we do then the experience can be so traumatising that family life is never the same again. No, this is an 'in case of emergency, break glass' situation.

The reconciliation might go something like this:

> *'When we live more peacefully, we have the energy to go out and do fun things. What sorts of things would you like to be doing? Shall we plan to go out at the weekend?'*

> *'I love spending time with you both. Remember the fun we had when we went to x?'*

Sibling on the receiving end

It may not be as simple as one sibling dishing out the violence and intimidation and one being on the receiving end, but if it is clear that this is pretty much what's happening, it is in my view important to support the latter, specifically and robustly. We must be honest with them and name what is going on.

> *This is abusive./That was violent./That was intimidating./You should not have to put up with it./It is frightening to live like this./It is not acceptable./I am going to deal with it./I am going to keep you safe./This is what I'm going to do.*

When violence is present in our homes, it's often the child with the violent behaviours who gets the attention. This is the child you talk about, think about, lie awake fretting about, talk to your social worker about. It can feel like swimming against a strong current but I think we must nevertheless shift our attention more towards the child/ren and perhaps other family members who are on the receiving end. If they have a tendency to 'just get on with it', if they 'disappear under the radar', if they tell you 'it's fine, I'm used to it' then our alarm bells should be ringing at full volume. Think about what you might say to a friend who shares with you that their partner is abusing them. Through living in a soup of violence and aggression I learned that when I had obviously lost control, when I exhibited helplessness and victimhood, things were a lot worse. I think our children feel unsafe when they are 'winning'. It's another of the great contradictions of trauma – 'I'm going to do everything in my power to overcome you, but if I do overcome you, we will both lose.' Time and again I had to take time out and re-educate and remind myself how to regain my power. That's no mean feat when you feel alone and under siege. It's the reason why the right professional can play an important role in helping parents to overcome violence in the home. Strong and supportive coaching and collaborative problem-solving, accepting that there are no certain solutions, can be a lifesaver.

CHAPTER 9

The Hard Stuff

The adolescent years can bring with them hard stuff that kicks the previously considered hard stuff into the long grass. It's true that we're no longer worrying about small children who might run in front of trucks or off the edges of cliffs; however, our adolescents are skilled at seeking out new and novel dangers. And whilst I'll never tire of hearing 'all teenagers do that'[1] it's a brave person who trots that one out around most of us. It's true that yes, most teenagers have horrendously messy bedrooms, don't study very hard, spend long amounts of time on their phones and can get 'into a sh**ty' at the drop of a hat, but I have to say that not that many that I know of explore quite the range of human behaviours that we have the pleasure of witnessing.

If you're not up for reading anything super-challenging about therapeutic parenting in general or fostering or adoption then you'll want to skip this chapter. It's written for those who are struggling with the scary stuff and for that reason it is to the point and doesn't duck the difficult questions. At least that's how I've set out to write it. And, as always, I've tried to be honest whilst offering some practical approaches and ways of thinking about s***. I think that's more useful than pretending none of this goes on.

---

1   That's a lie, and I'm bloody sick of it.

If you are sinking under some of this hard stuff, or perhaps under different hard stuff (it's a diverse buffet) then you absolutely must cut yourself some slack and acknowledge that what you are coping with is extraordinary.

Control

By now we probably understand why our loved ones need to exert so much control over the household. And we're probably at the stage where asking them if they'd like fish fingers or sausages for tea, or whether they'd like to watch The Bake Off[2] now or the following evening isn't going to be enough to give them the control they crave.

Having control over one's own life is one thing and most teenagers are exploring and learning about decision-making, choices and consequences but some of our trauma-brained teenagers seem to have faulty control systems that have gone into over-drive. They seek family and world domination and, by my reckoning, the more out-of-control they feel, the more control they try to exert over others. I never really understood controlling behaviour until I experienced it in my house. It's incredible: relentless, insidious, stealthy. It can make you feel as though you are going crazy, it can make you question your own perceptions and memory and take you to psychological places you never imagined. It's useful to remind ourselves that when a particular behaviour has this much power, it is usually about survival. Our children have learned that to relinquish control and to trust others to take care of their needs is way too risky. Their adolescent selves take this experience and some of them

---

2   You'll probably know it if you're in the UK, but in case you're not, this is *The Great British Bake Off*, a hugely popular television programme.

will take it to its extreme. If your adolescent is doing this then you have my sympathy.

The faulty control system not only fights for control over things that will provide a direct benefit, it fights over everything. EVERYTHING. It can feel like the priority is to get one over you, to prove you are wrong, stupid, crazy, forgetful, to make sure you are last, that your place in the household is slowly removed, that your belongings are disappeared, your sleep is disturbed, your food is eaten, your social life is disrupted. If transference is a real thing, then I've got a pretty good idea what it must feel like to be a neglected child, fighting for my right to exist. The problem is I'm not a neglected child and I can't afford to live in that psychological space. In the face of such an onslaught it's very difficult to maintain one's sense of power and agency and once we begin to lose those things, it's a race to the bottom. Our children can become more scared the more helpless we become and their need for control more extreme. It's a vicious circle. And there's a point at which a traumatised young person's controlling behaviour tips over into abuse.

'I'm going to make you feel as s**t and as out-of-control as I feel' is, I believe, at the root of many of these extremes. It's not done consciously, but it's no less powerful for that. What we must try is not to get caught up in the trauma and dragged under by it. Noticing how control is exacted, how it's used and its targets is important. Is control centred around particular times of the day, or particular resources such as food? Is control aimed at particular members of the family? Is it done secretly, so it sets family members against each other? Is it causing splitting between you and your partner? Try to nail it down. Write it down if you can and explore it with your partner, if you (still!) have one. Get it out in the open. In fact, write a list of the main contenders – those aspects of family life that are being unhealthily controlled and which you would like to find some ways of improving. If there are more than a few, you might want to rank them in order of the most troublesome.

Control can impact upon and infiltrate many aspects of our lives. I've hit on a few contenders and offer up some strategies for your consideration.

The crack of dawn

The word on the street is that teenagers' natural rhythm is to stay up late and sleep all morning. But what if this isn't the pattern our loved ones have at all? What if getting up early, then earlier, then even earlier, then ridiculously early is their way of controlling the household? I don't know about you, but I've lived with trauma for so long, I have the hearing of a bat. I can be woken up by an owl screeching several miles away. I can be woken up by the cat scratching itself in another room. There's no chance I'll sleep through a teenager's alarm going off at 5am. And once I know there is a teen loose in the house, once I've checked I have my purse by my bed, there's no way I can get back to sleep. Rather unhelpfully I don't really have an answer to this one, other than asking, reasoning and then pointlessly and pathetically pleading. What I have also resorted to is 'I can't pick you up after 10 o'clock tonight because I'm too tired'. I've also tried to share the burden with my partner, who could sleep through a fire alarm, so that hasn't been very effective. I've tried to chill over it and accept that said teen needs to prowl around the house at 5am, waking everyone up, but I wasn't very good at that. What I know for sure though is that the more I took against the behaviour, the worse it got and the cause was probably the increasing stresses and strains of school. I focused much of my energy on working with school to reduce the pressures there. We also tried not to enable the getting up early by doing things like ensuring the wifi didn't come on until much later. It goes without saying that despite the dawn chorus, we were still on the very verge of being late for school every day. That's control for you, no logic.

Late for school

It's the devil's own job trying to ensure everyone is ready in the morning and no one is late, especially if you are rather fanatical about being on time. My experience is that the more you show you care about something, the more likely it is going to be a focus for controlling behaviours. Moving around the house very slowly on purpose, yawning very obviously, pretending to have zoned out when you mention what time it is are all tactics designed to piss you off and illicit a reaction. I'm not going to suggest that you must never react because that would make me a raging hypocrite. I'm just suggesting that you recognise this as a pinch point in the day and you try your best not to feed the control. Practise appearing not to give a s**t. Try phrases such as 'Well, I won't get into trouble if you're late.' Shrug. If you really struggle with all this, like I did, then keep busy for the time it takes for everyone to try out all their infuriating tactics. Wash up, clean the floor, sort out the recycling. It's way easier to keep calm when our hands are busy. Try not to show what a massive inconvenience it is. I'd provide a lift if the bus was missed, but I'd make the journey really uncomfortable and sometimes I would refuse to give a lift for social reasons later in the week. And if there were consequences dished out at school for being late then so be it. That's mean, right? Maybe it is, but that's how I played it.

And yes, it can feel like you've lived a day already when it's not yet 8.30 in the morning. That's not because you're a flake, it's because this is a psychologically exhausting exercise, especially when it has to be endured day after day.

Three spoons or four?

This is a minor example, but I'll include it for amusement and because it's indicative of lots of different flavours of controlling behaviour. If like me you tried your best to feed your young family healthily and healthy eating is something you care about, then you will no doubt know that this becomes a great stick to beat you with. If your controlling teen enjoys standing right by you putting many spoons of sugar into their hot drink, then stirring it whilst smirking, then you will know there is nothing for it other than to IGNORE IT. I am terrible at ignoring things like this. I vow I will and I am partially successful, then one day, perhaps after I've been woken up five consecutive mornings at 5am I will snap. It's a win for the controlling behaviour, because after all that's what it was all along. It doesn't even like an overly sweet mug of coffee, so to add insult to injury, you'll probably end up retrieving it from under a pile of clothes at some point, carrying it back to the kitchen and scraping the crust of sugar out of the bottom of it. This must all make me sound terribly petty and untherapeutic, but it has been my relentless reality. There may be other things you care deeply about which you have had to learn to keep a lid on.

The uncompromising position

You may be familiar with the uncompromising statement that seeks to shift the burden associated with a lack of compromise onto your shoulders. Statements such as 'I don't like that bread any more' or 'I'm not using that soap' may have their roots in genuine dislike or they may be rooted in control. If all efforts to reach a compromise are thwarted then you may come face to face with an uncompromising position. You may then find yourself further boxed in with 'I only like fresh baguette and that's all I will eat' or 'I'll only wash with the expensive shower gel'. Oh yes, trauma can look a lot like raging entitlement.

There is a difference between making reasonable adjustments and being a sucker. Be especially vigilant for uncompromising positions that are designed (unconsciously) to exploit your existing concerns over, say, under-eating or lack of personal care. How far are you willing to bend and at what point will you hand the baton of responsibility for, say, their personal care to your loved one? Being a solid therapeutic parent isn't about having to visit the local craft boulangerie twice a day.

'You said I could!'
Living with trauma, and catching some of it, wreaks havoc with one's memory. When it's in full-on control mode, trauma cleverly uses our impaired memory and cognition to get its own way.

> *'What time can you drop me to X's house? Remember you said you would?'*
>
> *'Uh, did I?' you reply, searching through the dark memory vaults and registering vague alarm at the name X, whose house is not on your list of 'safe places I'm happy to leave my child'.*
>
> *'Yes, you definitely did. Can't you remember?!'*

Before you know it, you're driving your loved one to an unsavoury part of town wondering how on earth that happened. It might be only hours later that you realise you never had the conversation about giving a lift to X's house, let alone were asked your permission. Our lives can become so mentally jam-packed that we lose track. We're then left with the guilt that we never should have dropped our child at X's house and nightmarish imaginings of headlines in newspapers about a tragedy that was caused by parental laxity (yours).

Once you've been played a few times, you become better at detecting a scam. My advice is to build in thinking time. Don't get bounced into immediate decisions about anything. 'Just let me think about that' is a good phrase to have at the tip of your tongue.

Once the dust has settled and the front-page headlines haven't some to pass, it's always worth considering a follow-up conversation,

> 'You caught me on the hop earlier. I realise now I'd never have agreed to drop you there. Do you understand why?'

> 'Next time I'm going not going to respond immediately.'

This conversation is essentially about risk and keeping safe and of course we come up against the traumatised adolescent brain and its difficulties in assessing risk and the attachment-compromised adolescent brain and its preference for any friend, no matter how scary they are, over no friend. It's a force we will only be able to stand up against for a limited time, but I still think it's worth having these conversations because we never know, one day in the future they may fall into place.

'Gaslighting'

I hesitate to use the term 'gaslighting' to describe what I mean by strange, mind-altering, secretive behaviours that get you doubting yourself, but as a term it works for me. Gaslighting is much in the news right now and is used to describe a set of conscious actions that are designed to make a person feel as though they are going crazy. I'm not at all suggesting that our loved ones are cognitively, consciously, strategically planning their approach, but the effect is nevertheless the same, in my experience.

Creeping around the house, moving things, hiding things, jumping out on you, telling elaborate lies and making out you've given your permission for something when you never even had the conversation are all, in my opinion, gaslighting-type behaviours. Taken on their own, they sound like nothing.

- My toothbrush is covered in soap.
- My wedding ring has disappeared.
- I was coming out of the bathroom and someone jumped out and scared the life out of me (laughed excessively, then later in the day recounted the story to an assembled group encouraging them also to laugh).
- The radiator in my bedroom has been switched off.
- I can hear creeping on the landing.
- I found my mug in the pond.
- I am mocked when I mispronounce something or wear something different.

The insidious and cumulative effect of events such as these is horrendous. So too is trying to describe it to the average person. You get to understand what people experiencing coercive control must feel like.

What I've struggled with is how clever these behaviours can seem, whilst being carried out by a young person with impaired cognitive skills. I guess it's the canniness of trauma. My own defence has been to remove myself from the soup, physically and emotionally giving myself the opportunity to get some distance and perspective, keeping a written record of happenings so I can look back on them with a clearer mind and talking to others who get it. If you can manage to employ any or all of these strategies I think you may conclude you are not going crazy.

Regaining control

At the risk of being repetitive, if you are losing yourself in a mess of controlling behaviours then before you can unpick them you absolutely must take some time out of the house, away from the racket, so you can examine what's happening more forensically and less emotionally. Try to boil down what's going on. Identify the top two areas of control that you want to tackle. Recording them in writing can help to nail them down and will give you something to return to when clarity is slipping away. Decide on your approach and your strategies. Record these as well. From my experience, it's best not to take on too many different strategies, just a couple might be enough. And have a careful think about whether controlling behaviours have become worse due to any underlying issues: school, social media, birth family contact, a fall-out with friends, the time of year, a transition. It may be worth thinking about how to reduce the anxieties around these underlying issues as well. It may also be worth ripping the plaster off and getting some fresh air in there: 'I've noticed you've been hiding my things lately and you usually do that when you're worried about something. Let's work out what it is and how I can help.'

I need I need I need

The only word I know that adequately describes the unwavering relentlessness of a need is 'fixation'. What that's got to do with trauma I'm not entirely sure of, other than the drive to meet a need, even if that need is some jewellery, a vape or a box of stink bombs. Some of the drive could also be about obtaining things that an adolescent might think helps them to fit in, or appear popular in some way. In my experience, it will often be around things that we tedious parents disapprove of. Rebellion against parents is a standard adolescent thing. I think we can safely say that the rebellion thing can get taken to rather an extreme (yes, another one).

It's relatively easy to get your hands on anything given a few online skills, mainly the ability to tick the 'I am over 18' box, which doesn't take that much nous. We may be skilled at intercepting the postman but we will be no match for the doggedly determined. Before we know it, the parcels are being delivered elsewhere, the extra money given for Cake Day at school is being siphoned off and things are disappearing from the house, presumably to be sold.

In the heat of a fixation, there's nothing I know of that will stand in the way of a need. It's scary and disempowering. As always, the only conversations that stick take place away from the heat. I recommend naming the fixation, if that's what you want to call it. Notice it, call it out, be curious about it.

'What's that all about?'

'Help me understand that need, it's really powerful, it's like it takes you over.'

There may also be a controlling aspect to the need that centres on the pleading or demanding it is met. Ever get bombarded with texts and verbal requests to the point you will be driven to the edge of insanity? Me too. Take time out. Be clear and stand firm. Then say what you see and feel: 'You're bombarding me, it's not on and it's not going to work. There are better ways of asking me.'

Porky pies

Lying takes all sorts of different forms and some types of lying can make you feel as if you are losing your mind. They can be magnificently elaborate and detailed, dramatic, confusing and shocking. We may act based on them and then when the curtain is pulled back and the trickery is revealed the effect can be like having the rug pulled from under us.

I am a trusting and believing person, probably too trusting and believing for my own good, but there we go, we can only play with the hand we've been dealt. The process of opening up and becoming more empathic that we have gone through during our children's younger years is essential and praiseworthy, but I suspect it leaves us at greater risk of being taken for a ride in later years. We get so skilled at listening and taking our child's side that we forget our critical thinking. Critical thinking is essential during this time.

I experienced a sudden realisation of my gullibility during a residential writing course. While I was 'getting away from it all' and my guard was down, I swallowed a huge number of fantasies from another student. I really warmed to this person and my empathy lights were on full beam. When I recount the fantasies to myself now I cannot believe I was taken in. I thought I'd heard it all, I thought I could recognise a fantasy a mile away, I thought I was practised. But my guard was down. I came away feeling very foolish and more aware than ever of my weakened trauma-infected brain.

Our young people, who have experienced huge levels of trauma, can create a fancy world that satisfies a need in them, perhaps to have an engaging story to tell to a gathered, enraptured audience, a drama to re-enact, to remind themselves they are alive or to escape into a more interesting imagined life. And whilst all these reasons may make sense, there's no escaping the fact that to be on the receiving end can be mentally de-stabilising and distancing. I've grown to realise that if I feel like I've been manipulated in some way, then I probably have. It takes an awful lot of strength and presence of mind not to fall prey to the convincing lies of a fantasist and we can only hope to maintain these by practising enormous amounts of self-care. We need to remember who we are, to maintain a strong sense of ourselves.

I've been advised in the past to practise curiosity in the face of blatant lies, but I became unable to do this. The best I could manage was to remain neutral. Sometimes I could revisit the lies at a later point and remark that I sensed the truth wasn't to be found there and to guess at the reasons behind the lies.

A lesson I learned the hard way was to never react in response to a recounted event involving the dreadful behaviour of a third person. There's nothing worse than angrily firing off an email to someone, only to realise after the 'send' button has been pressed, that truth had gone missing. I say that, but in terms of trauma, I think that some kind of emotional truth is present, but it's not the truth as most of us would recognise it. This is something that a skilled therapist should be able to unpick and explore. We can try but I wonder whether, in being a party to the fantasy, we have already played too strong an emotional part in it.

The tragedy of living with a lot of fantasy is that it distances us from our loved one. We put in place an emotional 'air gap'. I don't see how we can't. At our best we might be able to explore a fantasy, say out loud why it doesn't seem right and how that makes us feel. That's very different from directly calling out a lie and I don't believe that's the right approach. 'That's a lie' will be heard as 'you're a liar and I don't believe anything you say'. The trauma computer often seems to take what we say and put it through a set of catastrophic algorithms. It will be no good pleading that you made no such accusation. I apologise for swearing but there's no other way of putting this – parenting an adolescent with raging trauma and problems with the truth can be a complete head f**k.

Resource control

I've never come across any research or writing to confirm this but in my experience it seems that whilst the traumatised child is focused on meeting their needs, for example their need for food, the brain of the traumatised adolescent tells them that as well as meeting their own needs, they must prevent others from meeting theirs. The need system goes into over-drive, gets out of control. It's almost as though your existence becomes a threat to theirs.

Food, hot water, dry towels, laundry facilities: all of these resources can start to seem as though they are in short supply. Every day is like Black Friday.

My only advice in the face of severe competition for resources is to try to remove yourself from the competition. Hide away your food treats, keep a dry towel in your bedroom, lock your money away. Maybe some other, less obvious things become targets, like shampoo, or make-up. Again, it may be possible to earmark yours and keep them away from general use. It can make life a bit of an a**e-ache, but it's much less draining than constantly discovering that what you need or want has been taken and used or even damaged.

The boot of your car, the garage, the salad drawer in the fridge, the space behind the dictionary on the bookshelf can all be useful places to stash things. Supply generous amounts of things like shampoo for general use and buy it cheap to avoid resentment on your part that money is being poured down the drain. The strategy here is not to care, or at least try really hard not to care.

In my experience, when a resource is perceived to be at risk of running low, frantic over-consumption will be triggered. Let's say that you ran out of milk once, about six months ago, and ever since, there has been a race to drink milk, pints and pints of it. Trauma must drink the milk before the milk runs out, which in itself causes the milk to run out. You can never buy enough of the stuff. It will drive you crazy.

Let's say you desire a cup of coffee and you reach into the fridge and pull out an empty four-pint bottle of milk, which was procured not 24 hours ago, and you lose all powers of therapeutic reasoning and you go off on one. This, my friends, is unavoidable. And do you know what? I think a good old-fashioned rant doesn't go amiss from time to time. It is, after all, really irritating when stuff like this happens, especially when it is on top of a hundred other happenings.

Splitting

It is not unusual for those of us parenting alongside our partners to experience splitting. Splitting is when our relationally damaged child tries to come between us, to break down our united front as a way of controlling the temperature of the house, of getting what they want, of seeking the comfort of messy relationships, of not feeling left out in the cold. It's easy to understand why splitting happens. It's less easy to spot what's going on when you're on the receiving end. I don't know the divorce rate amongst therapeutic parents but I wouldn't mind betting it is higher than average. We should be taught about splitting on our preparation courses. It's really important.

Splitting takes a number of evolving forms. It might be rejecting one of you outright and refusing to co-operate with the other, it might be coming between you by spreading dis-information and confusion or it might be jamming a crowbar between your different parenting styles and wiggling it around. At its extreme, splitting is manoeuvring one of you to disbelieve and take against the other, in favour of the child, and this, I think, is the most treacherous kind of splitting there is, for you and your partner, and for your child. It gives the child power over us and although our child craves that power, they fear it too.

Here are some lessons I've learned about splitting.

- If you are on the receiving end of secret looks, remarks, controlling behaviours that take place away from the eyes of your partner, then you must tell them what's going on, even if you think you're imagining it. Keep a written record of each occurrence.
- If your partner tells you they think they may be on the receiving end of such behaviours it is essential that you hear them out and believe them. Become vigilant and if you witness anything, call it out. 'What was that dirty look that you just gave Mum all about?' 'I don't like it when you're mean to Dad.' And likewise, your partner must call it out when they experience it, and you must back them up. It could go something like this: 'You just gave me a really dirty look and when Dad turned around you smiled as though nothing had happened. I don't like it,' followed by this from you: 'It's not acceptable to shoot Mum a horrible look and then hide it from me, I don't like you treating Mum like that.' Then be prepared for categorical denial, which you must stand firm against together.
- Beware that your child may behave entirely differently with the two of you; mean and spiteful towards one, cute and adorable towards the other. If you only see 'cute and adorable' it may seem unbelievable that what your partner tells you they are experiencing is real. So either your partner is a liar, or you are living with a child who has learnt to survive through managing the adults around them. Which is most likely?

- If you are living at the hard end of this and no one believes you, then keep your phone in your pocket set to record. If you capture evidence, play it back to your partner and, if appropriate, to a professional. You really shouldn't have to collect evidence to prove your point, but the power of survival has conned many an intelligent, well-balanced person.

- If your differing parenting styles is the soil in which the splitting grows, you absolutely must do some therapeutic parenting training together. It might be that one of you is trained up to the eyeballs and one of you has to work for a living. Taking a couple of days off work and doing some training may just be the best investment you can make in the future and in family harmony. Go into it with an open mind. Try not to assume that therapeutic parenting is a heap of bulls**t.

- Regularly share with each other the ways in which splitting is taking place. Support each other. Believe each other. Try really hard not to apportion blame. Splitting is mega-powerful and is only defeated when safe adults work together.

- Voice to your child that you stand together, all of you, and that you and Mum/Dad are a strong team. You may even need to say that you and Mum/Dad tell each other things and don't keep big secrets from each other in order to make sure you can work as a team and that things run smoothly around the house. Be careful not to make this show of unity seem like you are excluding your child (this may be their default position). 'We both love you. Group hug.'

Aggressive and violent behaviours

There is growing evidence to show what many of us know from bitter experience: children are impacted greatly by exposure to toxic levels of stress both pre- and post-natally. It's little comfort that we were right all along, especially those whose children were taken into care at only a few weeks old (how can they possibly be impacted by trauma?) but at least the biological processes around toxic stress and other factors such as pre-natal exposure to alcohol are becoming better understood. There is now no denying that babies and children born into frightening, neglectful and violent environments can find it difficult to self-regulate. That's a science-y, polite way of saying that they may find themselves at the mercy of extreme emotional storms, including violent ones. If you live with a violent young person then you will know what this amounts to, in full surround sound and Technicolor.

Living with the violent behaviours of a young child is horrendous enough; living with the violent behaviours of a hulking great teenager is something else. And it's all well and good understanding why our teenager is violent, but that doesn't help much when we are on the receiving end of terrifying behaviour and when we fear for our safety and that of our family.

It doesn't take much exposure before we are tiptoeing around, feeling generally anxious all of the time, avoiding certain situations and conversations and experiencing hyper-vigilance. Living like this is exhausting and soul-destroying. When we witness or are on the receiving end of violence, it is utterly terrifying and nothing can prepare you for it. There is no other part of my life in which I have ever thought to myself, 'Someone might get seriously hurt here', but I have thought that plenty of times as a therapeutic parent. It kicks into action our own fight/flight/freeze response and as a result we can behave in ways we never thought we were capable of.

I've found that the language used to talk about violence can serve to reduce the impact of it and, in a way, to sterilise it. For example, damage to and destruction of our homes and valued possessions gets translated as 'damage to property'. Then there's verbal abuse that might be described as 'threats' or 'intimidation'. Neither sound that significant, that traumatic. Why are we such bags of nerves? Why aren't we coping? Do we need to set firmer boundaries? Go on a parenting course? 'I'd never stand for such behaviour' we hear from others. How about this as a different way of describing violent behaviours:

> 'He smashed our television by throwing our son's school bag at it. The sound was terrible. He was screaming, "You f***ing b******d I'm going to f***ing kill you, I'm going to rip your f***ing eyes out." I was scared he was going to turn on his brother and punch him. He was blocking our way out of the room so we were trapped. Then he turned to me, ran at me so he was a few centimetres from my face and raised his fist and shouted, "And don't think you're going to get away without being beaten, you c**t". I stayed as calm as I could and kept repeating, "Get out, get out" but it just enraged him even more. His face changed and he said in a really chilling voice, 'Why? Are you scared of me? You pathetic wh**e.' I can't really remember what happened after that but he ran out and we could hear him smashing up something upstairs. We ran out of the house and to our neighbour's house. We were both shaking so badly. After that I felt completely numb and exhausted, like I just couldn't function at all. I am tired of living like this. Nothing makes it better. It's hopeless.'

If you live with a violent young person then you won't need any of this explaining. You may, however, feel the need to lend this book, or photocopy these pages and pass them to a family member, a trusted friend, or a professional. You may want me to point out that unless you have lived with a violent young person, you have no idea how it feels or how you would react. And those of us who have experienced it are rendered mute. Trauma (because this is what living with a violent person is) leaves us lost for words to describe what our lives are like and it disrupts our memories. This makes us unable to represent ourselves well, to make a good account of ourselves and leaves us open to (mis)judgement. And because most people have luckily never had to face real violence they are able to indulge in fantasies about what they would say and do should they be in that situation. Let's just say that real and fantasy violence are very different and believe me, you wouldn't have half the courage or presence of thought that you think you would ('I'd never stand for that in my house', oh, really).

If you are supporting a parent living with violence, either in a personal or professional capacity then the best thing you can do is listen to them and believe them. If they appear spaced out and confused, or bitter and angry then consider that this might be what trauma has done to them and that they are not the confident, happy person they once were. I have included a chapter called 'Supporting Families' that goes into more detail.

Living with violence is extremely traumatising. Trauma is catching. Trauma gradually reduces our capacity to help our young person out of their trauma. The more traumatised we become, the more dysregulated our young person becomes. If we're not careful, it becomes a miserable race to the bottom. Trauma really does hold the majority of the cards. If you find yourself in this situation then here are a few suggestions.

Tell someone about it

Tell your social worker, your good friends, trusted family members, neighbours (the nice, understanding ones). You need help with this. It is too big to cope with on your own. You also need support. Sharing the shit over half a cider can help lighten the load. It can also expose us to other people's incredulity. We can find ourselves normalising the most terrible events and that's not always helpful. Sometimes we need to keep a hold of how extreme this all is. It's really not OK to live like this.

Get therapeutic help

If you are living with violent and aggressive behaviours then your social worker should be checking in with you regularly. I would also strongly advise that you seek out good quality therapeutic help for your child and for yourself. Good therapists will take you as a package and work with you together and separately. In my opinion it is best to start therapy before things are really terrible, but I realise that this isn't always achievable. Things may have to hit the scary rock bottom before our young people agree to accept help and before services become available.

Work out a safety plan

A safety plan sets out what action you will take when violence hits. It sounds more formal then anything I managed. Ours wasn't even written down. It was succinct and easy to remember. Who has time to read a document when there's an ironing board aimed at your head? At the least, answer these questions: Where will you go? Who will you call on? How will you keep siblings protected? Who will you call for help? If the violence is serious then your best bet might be to get the hell out of there. You also need to decide at what point you will call the police. More on that a bit later. The safety plan needs to be shared with all members of your family, including the young person themselves. I think this is best done in a no nonsense, no blame way. Ideally we'd like our young person to regulate themselves, or at least to remove themselves, but when their brains have gone to Code Red, they aren't thinking and they probably won't recall the plan. However, reminding everyone of the plan when times are calm is a good way of reinforcing it:

> *'Can you remember where you go if you feel the anger rising?'*
>
> *'To my room?'*
>
> *'Exactly. Well done.'*

I learned that it is particularly powerful to share the plan with siblings. It is a strong sign that you have their safety in mind and that you have some control. Initiating the conversation alone can result in more conversations about living with violence. Other children in our homes must not come to think that putting up with it is the only course. We model what it is to take back power in a controlled and intelligent way and that's a valuable skill for life.

Explore the triggers

Violence can of course come out of nowhere, or out of a unique set of events that unravel very quickly or can take place at certain times of the day or be triggered by certain events. It may be that the time after coming home from school is particularly risky, or that having to hear a negative response to a request lights the blue touch paper. More general disappointment or shame may also be a trigger: perhaps a friend didn't want to come out or a piece of tech is broken. Pinpointing the triggers can get us thinking about how to avoid or reduce the impact of them. If our young person is able to I think it's worth exploring this with them involved and with shame turned right down. We're aiming to encourage their thinking skills and buy-in.

In the heat of the moment

Once violent has blossomed, it's pretty impossible to do or say anything to reduce it. It's very easy, as you know, to make things worse. We've all leaned into the violence and accepted its invitation and we must forgive ourselves for that (after all we have a fight/flight/freeze response too). Ideally we must try to step away, not say anything other than what's planned, for example, 'I'm going to go outside until the coast is clear'. Anything we do say has to be short and not repeated over and over. The dysregulated trauma brain will probably not take in what we've said anyway, or may misinterpret it in a negative way. My planned statements in response to a direct and real physical threat have been 'I'm going to remove myself somewhere safe' or 'Get outside now' or 'Back off'. I will assume as much physical presence and confidence as I can muster. If things get really serious I will say 'If you hurt anyone I will call the police'. When it is possible and I'm not blocked in, I or we leave, again with confidence. (Running away with fear, although not always avoidable, can, I think, escalate the situation.) It takes a fair amount of nerve to walk away from this, especially if you think the young person might come after you, but it gets easier with practice. You get to know how this violence business operates. If the violence is then enacted on your house and its contents, again this comes down to a judgement call. If the destruction is being wrought on their things then inevitably they will have to sit with the consequences of that. If our young person is out of control and for example smashing windows, televisions, cars then in my book that warrants a call to the police. Sometimes we may have to ask ourselves: how bad would it have to get before we call the police? We all have different tolerances. I'm a great believer in thinking through these scenarios before I find myself in one of them and when half of my brain has shut down. I'm also a believer in talking through the scenarios with my loved one, as part of the shared safety plan.

De-escalation

What we're really aiming for is to avoid the violence blossoming in the first place. When we see it gathering on the horizon we might find that our young person tries to engage us in a conflict. Unless I'm very unusual, I think it can be incredibly hard to resist the engagement, particularly if it is some kind of enraging statement, which is probably designed to register on our trigger scale. My 'go to' responses to stop myself from leaping in are 'I really don't want an argument', 'You seem to want a fight. I'm not up for that today', 'I'm going to walk away and do something else because I don't want an argument', 'Help yourself to some crisps instead'. Some of our young people will be so desperate to raise the temperature that they might follow us. We can try to keep busy: 'I need to brush the floor.' To keep ourselves safe we may not want to turn our backs. If violence comes closer then we may need to say 'remember the plan' and if that doesn't catch it in time then we will have to act on the plan. I must point out that I am not that experienced in the finer points of de-escalation because basically not much that I tried worked. Chew some peanuts? Bounce on the trampoline? Punch a cushion? Yeah, OK.

Buy yourself time

If our young person wants something from us and we sense that if they don't get the answer they want then there is a risk they will react violently then buying ourselves time can be an effective strategy. It's easy to get 'bounced' into making a decision, particularly when we are living in a pressure-cooker of emotions. 'I need time to think about it' and 'I need time to talk it over with Mum/Dad' are useful phrases to have at our fingertips. If our need to buy time isn't accepted then I think it's all right to say 'If you keep hassling me the answer will definitely be no.' If you have to deliver a 'no' then the timing can be planned in advance, for example when you are not alone in the house, or when a sibling isn't in the firing line.

Risky conversations
When a complicated situation presents itself and we have to say something to our young person that we know they will find difficult we can find ourselves feeling highly anxious and avoidant. I've learned to recognise this in myself and nudge myself into recognising that this is something that needs 'outing'. 'I need to talk to you about something important and I think it might make you feel angry. I want to have a grown-up conversation about it with you and not have to worry that you're going to get angry' may be a useful way of doing the groundwork. If you find car journeys regulate your young person, or being outdoors, then these are options.

Loosen up
When we live in constant conflict we can become rigid and inflexible in our thinking. It's not our fault, it's just the way it is. My rigidity is me saying 'no' to things a lot. Sometimes I find myself saying 'no' to perfectly reasonable requests. I try hard to say 'yes' whenever I can, or at least 'let me think about that'. Making decisions when your brain is hovering over the 'fight/ flight/freeze' button is generally a bad idea (and the reason why

we have to carry out a lot of mental preparation and rehearsals for how we need to behave during a violent episode).

Find good-quality support

Seek proper, well-informed help and support. There are more courses and approaches available now such as Non-Violent Resistance and most courses on therapeutically parenting teens will cover violent behaviours. Find a therapist who can support your young person and you. This should not be unfamiliar territory for well-qualified, experienced therapists. It may be worth checking before you start on a course of therapy. It's important that a therapist understands the links between trauma and violent behaviours and shame. Your young person may benefit from learning about that too. It may start to shift their belief that they are bad. You may have a social worker who really gets trauma and violent behaviours and that person will be a great asset. If your social worker doesn't get it, then I would go to the head of department and (calmly) ask that they consider assigning you a social worker who is experienced and confident in that aspect of supporting therapeutic parents (yeah, I know they should all be, but the fact is some aren't and I don't need to tell you how damaging it is to be supported by someone who isn't adequately qualified).

Family meeting

A meeting can be a way of making a clear statement in a formal way. It may be something that involves family members only, or a professional or a friend as well. It is important that everyone knows how this thing is going to work and the messages that are going to be delivered. It needs to feel important and significant but not shaming. I've set out how the family meeting might run in the chapter 'Siblings'. Or your young person may completely refuse to take part. None of these strategies are silver bullets and we shouldn't feel like failures if they don't come off.

A family meeting can be a useful strategy if you find yourselves in a spiral of violence, when no one can get their heads above water long enough to take a breath before the next wave hits. It is crucial that any kind of intervention such as this isn't one massive exercise in public shaming. Inviting other family members, neighbours, friends or whatever may prove too much for our young person who may quickly tip into shame and from there into fight/flight/freeze. I'm not saying we should keep the fact that violence is happening in our homes a secret because that is damaging too, but just that we may have to take care that when we involve someone outside the immediate family it is someone our young person trusts, who is skilled, like perhaps a therapist. This is not a time to take a risk on someone.

The messages we are looking to share are: this is awful for all of us and we need to work out a better way to live alongside each other. All members of the family who are able need to express how this is for them. Then there must be agreed strategies. If our young person runs out then when the family is re-regulated you may try again. If we play along with the avoidance then we may just feed the cycle of violence. But as I said, this is only one way of going about things. A car journey or a quiet outdoor space are alternative venues for delivering these messages but only if they work in your family.

Calling the police
Calling the police is not something that should be taken lightly, nor should it be avoided altogether. I'm not a fan of constantly threatening to call the police and extrapolating what might happen if you did. But if members of your family are getting punched, kicked, their hair pulled, if your home is being

terrorised, set alight, if serious threats are being made, then you must seriously consider calling the police. It's a hard step to take and it might help to consider what the fallout would be if a sibling, for example, was seriously hurt and we hadn't sought assistance. We have a duty to keep everyone in our family safe and we must take that duty seriously.

We may need to call the police on the emergency, or the non-emergency, line, depending on the situation. It may feel terrible. It may also be a tremendous relief. The police are used to dealing with violent behaviour and your teenager won't be the first they've come across (they may be the first in a home like yours, but don't let that concern you). The involvement of the police sends a strong message to our young person that enough is enough. It doesn't mean they are going to be criminalised, but that you are no longer prepared to tackle this alone. Once the police have visited your home, more services should get involved. It raises the game.

Be prepared for your young person to be anything but apologetic in front of the police. They may behave as though they don't care and may even be unbelievably rude. It's horrible to witness but it is worth remembering that they are terrified but don't feel safe enough to show their vulnerability. It's an act.

Repair
After any big incident, the important part is the repair. We may all prefer to crawl away to our respective spaces and forget about everything but this can create an awful lot of unfinished business. Our child's shame levels will be sky high and if we can't muster up the courage to talk over the incident and put it to bed that may only prove that the incident is indeed too shameful to talk about, or to even think about. Another awful incident is buried away to fester.

In my experience there is little point raking over things when emotions are still high. I would, however, communicate that it will be talked over at a later point. When our children were little, we may have moved quickly to repair, but our older children, I think, need to learn to sit with uncomfortable feelings. They will also spot our faked repair a mile off. No, I think we all need time to regroup after a horrible event. They may find that still time very difficult to manage and may try to cajole us back, by making light or joking around. It's fine to say, 'I'm not ready to laugh about that. I'm still hurting.'

The repair itself is along the good old lines of 'you're a good person who did a bad thing' but not perhaps in those terms (doesn't the therapeutic language get stale and meaningless?). I like to be straightforward and 'clean' about what happened and I like the 'before, during and after' approach. This is a way of framing the incident inside a positive normality:

> *'You were doing OK, you helped me unpack the shopping, then something set you off. What was that again?'*

They probably won't remember, or be able to say it out loud.

> *'It is completely unacceptable to threaten or terrorise anyone like that. You were completely out of control. It is NOT OK.'*

Allow a space.

> *'Your brother was terrified. No one deserves to be terrified in their own home. This is where we are meant to feel safe.'*

> *'I love you, OK.'*

Space.

> *'It's not right to behave like this.'*

Space.

> *'I get that you were angry. We have to find better ways for you to deal with those massive feelings. It's not all right to spill them over everyone else.'*

You may have An Arguer, who has to butt in and divert you off course. Be vigilant and keep on the path you've laid out. If they really won't let you continue, it's OK to say, 'You're not ready for this conversation now, we'll have it later.'

In my view, repair has to involve a reiteration of the strategies your young person is meant to be using, going to their room, running outside, whatever that is. The safety plan has to be mentioned. It's kind of an exercise in examining what went wrong and how we can help to prevent it going wrong again.

We can then help our loved ones to do something nice for everyone and to apologise. They may not be able to do this without a lot of support.

If you and your young person are both taking part in therapy then this may be the ideal time to begin helping them to understand where the anger comes from so that they can be supported to see it in the context of their early experiences. Ideally we'd like them to feel safe enough to feel anger at what happened to them and to allow sadness and grief to move in. Only then might they allow us to comfort and nurture them.

—

Tackling violent behaviours as a parent has so much to do with avoiding conflict, extinguishing fires (metaphorically) and keeping things cool. In proper words that's called 'self-regulation'. Self-regulation is supremely difficult in the face of rage, full-on violence and verbal horribleness. I think it's made out to be easier than it is. It is much more difficult when we are worn out. We absolutely must allow ourselves time to recover after incidents and to rebuild our energy and our hope for the future. Do not scrimp on self-care.

What's mine is yours

If your child takes things, food, money, things that belong to you, and you find it infuriating, enraging, worrying and all the other triggers then it's really important to get familiar with where the need to take things is coming from. It is a need, an unconscious drive and that's something that can be hard for us to get our heads around.

He or she steals, he or she takes things, hoards, gathers. There are lots of ways of describing this with varying amounts of catastrophising. It can appear to be well planned, which can con us into believing that it is coming from a cognitive part of the brain, which can lead us on to thinking that our child is some kind of master criminal in the making. I don't think they are. We're not talking about the Brink's-Mat robbery here. Trauma-related behaviours such as taking things have a habit of appearing to be much better planned than they are.

I rarely leave my bag unattended, but if I do it will be raided very quickly. Like I said, trauma is quite incredible at masking itself to be super-computer clever. The same child may not be able to tell the time or recite a times table. Survival intelligence is an interesting thing and I haven't come across anything that accurately accounts for it. It's the lower brain in cognitive clothing. It's like my bag and me both have GPS trackers attached and when we are parted a silent message is sent to the traumatised brain. 'You've got five minutes, raid me, and keep the noise down'.

I am familiar with the reasons why things get taken and hoarded. Our children have learnt not to trust that we can take care of them and they have learned to rely on things for comfort rather than relationships. None of this knowledge holds back the intense feelings of annoyance, betrayal and damaged trust that I feel when I go into my bag and discover that money is missing. I feel it in my body. My heart kind of sinks a bit. I feel angry at whoever I suspect of taking the money and at myself for being so stupid as to leave my bag around. When I make a discovery I've learned that I absolutely must not react straight away. What I often do is react straightaway.

Our therapeutic capabilities increase greatly after a night's sleep. It's like composing an angry email – always sleep on it before pressing 'send'. So my first piece of advice is to wait a while, let yourself calm down, think about your strategy.

The most important part of the strategy is to be absolutely, 100 per cent certain that something has been taken and that you know who has the light fingers. Once you've established the facts and discounted any uncertainty, here are some ideas that you might want to consider:

Say nothing
If it's a minor offence, if you have bigger mountains to climb, if there's a risk of destabilising a precious and hard-won calm then consider saying and doing absolutely nothing.

Hide valuables away
If the money or whatever is locked away and can't be taken then the chances of our child taking from us and suffering the subsequent fallout and shame are significantly reduced. There's little point putting temptation in the way of our dysregulated and impulsive children.

Be vigilant

Keep your bank and credit cards safe, make sure your child is looking away when you put your PIN into the cashpoint, password protect all your computers and beware of saving payment details on 'buy now' websites. Our kids may struggle with cognitive skills but that doesn't necessarily hold them back from achieving the most astonishing security breaches. That's the survival brain, prioritising the skills required to hack into your bank account over long division and fractions. If only there were a degree course in financial stealth there would be top marks all over the place.

Go with the hoarding

Many of our children hoard food and other items. Infuriating though this can be, I've yet to come across a strategy that works, other than the long, hard job of building safety and security. Again, we can reduce the opportunities for excessive hoarding by not having lots of crappy food in the cupboards and by acknowledging and accepting the drive to hoard. Get equally as canny with your own hoarding. There's nothing like retrieving a sneaky Creme Egg from the boot of your car of an evening to soothe away the struggles of the day.

Consider airing the hoarding in a non-judgemental way. Explore why it is you think the hoarding takes place and agree a way forward together, for example: 'I've noticed you hoard food for the night-time. You experienced long, hungry nights when you were a baby. Maybe it's to do with that. How about I make you a snack to eat before bed?'

By accepting and understanding the drive to hoard we hope to reduce shame and increase trust and safety. We also step away from the control battle.

Strategic taking

Let's say that something really precious of yours disappears, like perhaps your wedding ring. Maybe you took it off before you washed up, or left it in the bathroom. Not there? Then you get that horrible sinking feeling that your wedding ring has been taken and that you will never see it again.

It's very difficult to get all playful, accepting and curious about such incidents. I can't manage it, even though I know that straightforward anger and threats will only reduce the chances of me being reunited with my, let's say, just as an example, wedding ring.

After moving through a number of different emotions I managed a clean(ish): 'Look, I think you took my ring. Tell me where it is. I'll try my best not to be cross about it.'

The shame and fear of me being abusive (which I've been proving I'm not for a VERY long time now) made it impossible for the disclosure to be made. I found it eventually, somewhere safe, but odd.

Taking such items is a symbolic act in itself, I think. Perhaps I should have found it within myself to explore the reasons why something that represents my relationship with my husband should have been squirrelled away, but after searching the house and contorting my hand around the U-bend of the kitchen sink I really didn't feel like it.

If you suspect your engagement or wedding rings will be taken, the advice of the great and the good is to never take them off. Yeah, OK. PERHAPS I'LL LIVE IN A SEPARATE HOUSE SOMEWHERE SO I CAN KEEP MY THINGS SAFE THEN. Sorry, I don't know what came over me just then. What a massive over-reaction.

Air it

The 'air it' strategy runs through so much of this secretive shameful behaviour and taking things is no different. We do our best to understand the roots of the behaviour, to empathise, and then we open up a conversation.

> *'I understand why you do it and I don't think you even mean to. Is that right?'*
>
> *'I'm going to help you by trying harder to keep things out of sight.'*
>
> *'Try to tell me when you're feeling tempted.'*
>
> *'You're stressed about X at the moment so that might be why you're taking more.'*

It's not OK

Despite the lovely acceptance and all the rest of it, there comes a point when it really is not OK to steal money and belongings from other people. If the behaviour is persistent then I think it's worth keeping up with the strategies and adding on harder consequences.

> *If you take money you either return it, or do something to earn it back. If you take someone's valuable belonging you return it or you do something to earn the money to buy another one. I'm cross that my ring has disappeared and I need some time on my own. It's really precious to me and I can't believe it's gone. Don't cosy up to me, I need it back.*

The key to this approach is to keep up a firm, calm, clean approach. No hysterics.[3]

---

3   Note to self.

There may come a time when we need to involve outside agencies and we may no longer be able to avoid the involvement of the police. Taking money from other people, perhaps visitors to the house or from people outside the home and from shops can ramp up the response required. We hope to have done enough to avoid this, and if we can't we must remember that it's not our fault. Sometimes a hard message needs to be sent and sometimes that must come from a police officer, a head teacher or a boss. In the real world, there are consequences and there is no avoiding them. Where we come in is in catching our young person if they do crash into real-world consequences with empathy and support, but not excuses.

The Crisis Cycle

The Crisis Cycle is something I've observed and been entangled in many times. I don't know if it's a real, researched thing, but describing and analysing it has helped me and mine to get our heads around some really messy shit. Its identification came about because one day I said out loud, 'We bounce from one crisis to another' and Mr D, an engineer (aeronautical), drew this:

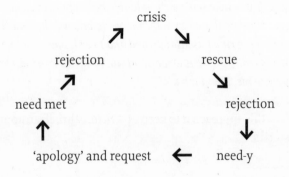

There is no start or end to the Crisis Cycle, but for ease of explaining, let's start with the crisis itself.

Crisis

Serious trouble at school, trouble with the police, or both at the same time, or racking up an online debt, or running off to meet a stranger, or smashing something up in the house, or threatening to batter someone in the house, or posting something unbelievable online. You get the drift. More than the average. Something that drains the heart and soul out of family life for a good few days.

Rescue

Rescue takes place when we liaise with school or the police, or both, pay off the debt, respond to the risk, reaffirm boundaries, enact our safety plan. We become the rescuers. During the rescue there may be a state of quiet, shocked truce that might even feel more pleasant than 'normal' family life. It might feel kind of nice to be needed and to be able to do something active for a change, rather than just soak in a puddle of our own despondency.

Rejection

'You idiots, you rescued me and I hate that you had to do that' is probably what the post-rescue rejection is all about. It won't come out like this though, will it? It'll be rude and offensive and eventually vile.

Need-y

The one big flaw in being vile to your parents becomes apparent when you need something like, let's say, a lift, some money, a haircut, some new trainers, an iTunes voucher. Oh dear. You'd better start sucking up to them.

Hollow apology

'Sorry.'

'Sorry for what?'

'Just for last week.'

'For what last week?'

With hardly a breath drawn before...

The request
The request makes complete sense of the apology. The request is about having needs met, however that can be achieved. The request may come when your guard is down and may play into your weak spot. You may be encouraging a friendship with Potential Friend B. 'Can I go to Potential Friend B's house on Friday, we're going to do something wholesome that you'd approve of.' Immediate rejection may follow the need being met.

The request may be the next crisis in disguise.

Crisis
Back there again, and so it continues.

If you are being swept around and around here are a few ways you might interrupt the cycle.

Identify it
This is easier if you keep some kind of a diary. It doesn't matter how scrappy it is. Think about all the recent crises, and how each built and unravelled. Share it with your partner, if you (still) have one.

Slow it down

Think about the part you play in the cycle, as rescuer and satisfier of needs. Could you stand back from the crisis more? Could you hold back the repair and sit in the discomfort of disrepair for longer as a way of slowing the cycle down? Could you voice what's happening and perhaps say out loud what you think will come next? 'I think you're going to try to make up with me soon because the weekend is coming and you'll want a lift somewhere. No? OK, maybe I'm wrong.' 'Is this a real "sorry" or a "sorry I want something"?' Perhaps show your child the cycle, in whichever way will make most sense. Describe what's going on to your child. You could say things like 'I see you bouncing from crisis to crisis, drama to drama and it must be exhausting'.

Describe the rescue, the need, all of it. You can say 'this is what I see happening'. This is the ultimate 'say what you see' strategy.

Plan

You will know what calms choppy waters in your house: a tech break, more family time, less freedom for a while. This isn't carried out punitively. We are aiming to give everyone a chance to sit still, allow the calm back in and to build in enough thinking time so that our child isn't bouncing from crisis to crisis. Should you consider just saying 'no' to a few things? Is it OK that everyone's week is screwed up and then Crisis Child gets to go out on Friday night with £25 in their pocket?

Take out some of the emotion

Really consider whether the crises are yours or theirs. Could you allow them more space to feel the full effects of their crises? Could you practise the Therapeutic Shrug of Not My Problem more often? Could you try a 'You've got yourself into a right mess, good luck sorting it out? Fancy a lemonade?' Be present but allow the police officer or the teacher to say what they need to, without protecting our child from it. Let them experience the exclusion, the hangover, the friendship breakdown. These are real-world natural consequences.

Be prepared for some push-back because you are not playing the part assigned to you. It's often only when our children feel the frozen winds that they start to make choices that will protect them from frostbite.

The Crisis Cycle, if indeed it is 'a thing' owes much, I suspect, to the adolescent brain with its need for thrill-seeking, danger and its (even more) reduced ability to fathom out consequences, plus the early, messy way of doing relationships model, with its drive towards having needs met and controlling significant adults. Understanding the cycle is one thing and it's useful to do that. Living with it, being grabbed by the hair and spun around and around until you don't know what day it is or which way is up, is something else. Try not to be an actor in these tragedies and take massive care of yourself.

Unwise friendships

I could patronise you with soapy bubbles about how horrible friends are just innocent kids, with difficult home lives and struggling parents. All that is probably true, but when your teenager is gravitating towards the group you wouldn't choose for them in a million years, it becomes a lot more difficult to play the inclusive, permissive parent (I find that those who broadcast the inclusive friends line are usually those who will never find themselves having real-life experience of it).

We know why our children make poor friendship choices (is that a gentler way of putting it?). Their untraumatised, well-adjusted peers find them maybe immature, a bit unusual, a bit 'over-the-top', or shy and withdrawn. This leaves our children fishing in a small pond and they are, let's face it, attracted to wayward, exciting kids who are a bit of a laugh in school and who take risks and are allowed out at all hours of the day and night. These kinds of relationships are by their nature quite shallow and undemanding in terms of attachment. When they do begin to make healthier friendships they perhaps haven't yet got the skills to maintain them. There may be a lot of falling out and some of it might be rather catastrophic. I've found myself saying over and over, 'It might be better not to be friends with X.' It makes no difference. At the end of the day, it's better to have an awful friend rather than a dull friend or no friend at all.

Not all of our children struggle quite this much, of course. Some can experience hurt and rejection, learn, move away and find better friendships. It's lovely when this happens. And like all teenagers, ours are experimenting with who they are, what they enjoy doing, and can transition through and beyond friendships while they are doing this.

For those who really struggle with peer relationships though, peer influence can be a huge source of awfulness and we may witness an endless stream of 'friendships' blowing through our family life. And during peak adolescence, when young people naturally and gradually move away from family and towards a supportive peer group, it can spell real trouble. There are two trouble spots for our teens: first, they probably won't make this transition gradually, and second, they won't have a supportive, safe peer group to bounce into. Oh, bother.

There are many aspects of my family life that set me apart from my non-therapeutic parent peers and one of those is the parts of town I now know like the back of my hand. If there's a crumbling house with rotting beds outside it and a drunk man wearing a string vest sat on the front step, I've been there. I know, again, not very politically correct. Excuse me. But would you leave your child there, for a sleepover? We can find ourselves making very tough choices indeed, and then we may find ourselves having no control over the situation at all. I won't share this here, but if you ever meet me, ask me about prom night. What a high point that was.

Here are some things I have discovered that help sometimes and don't help other times.

Entertain at home

Making it clear your home is somewhere your child can bring friends back to can be a way of reducing the chances they will gravitate towards string vest man's house. This might not work for as long as you hope it will. String vest man allows all sorts of carry-on that you wouldn't in your house and for that reason it will have a pull that a few tubes of Pringles, a barbecue and Netflix won't. Do it while it works.

Play taxi driver

Without wishing to fall into more stereotyping, I frequently found myself the only car-driving adult able to transport a group of teenagers to wherever they wanted to go and back. I carried out this role when I could, even when I was muttering under my breath about why it was always me. Again, it allowed me to hold on to some control and knowledge about where they were going and with whom.

Say 'no'

There are some adults in our communities that aren't safe for our young people to be around. Saying 'no' to 'can I go to X's house?' or worse still 'can I have a sleepover at X's house?' is necessary on occasion, if not without enormous fallout. Our children may reach an age when no matter what we say, they are going to go where they want to. I still think it's important for us to voice our concern. There may come a time when our concern rings in their ears. If they must feel the danger before they can acknowledge it then we will have to be prepared to welcome them home to safety, nurture and 'that must have felt scary'. While 'I told you so' obviously won't work, a bit of 'I did try to warn you' might not go amiss.

Thinking skills

If it's possible to still have the 'what might happen if' type conversation then go for it. What might happen if X's dad is drunk? What might happen if you can't get home? What might happen if they leave you? What might happen if X gets caught shoplifting and you're with him? This approach shows considered concern and demonstrates predictive thinking without the lecture.

Keep disapproval private

It goes without saying that if you have a child who goes out of their way to do the opposite of what you want them to, even if it isn't really what they want, then take care with expressing negative opinions about friends. In fact, take care with that anyway. It may have the opposite effect to that which you intend. The exception is when a 'friend' is being clearly vile towards your child, but even then we must tread carefully. 'I don't like the way she treats you' can be a good starter.

What is a friend?

To you and me, a friend is someone we know well and like and that we see often or from time to time. To our attachment messy loved ones, a friend can have a whole different meaning. A friend might be someone they've been messaging on social media who could be a 17-year-old female, or could equally be a 65-year-old male with a criminal record for sexual offences against children. I'm a fan of initiating conversations about what a friend is. Be prepared to have everything you thought to be obvious, challenged.

One of the golden rules that should be obvious, but which isn't is 'don't go and meet someone you don't know in real life'. The risks our young people can and do expose themselves to on this front are eye-watering. Be vigilant. If you have reasonable suspicions contact the police. If our young people have reached 18 then it goes without saying that they can meet whoever they want to but that's not to say that they're not vulnerable.

Family life take-over

This might not work in your family, but it did in ours during a crucial time in early adolescence. When plans are being made that you know are not sound, that keep you awake at night, consider surprising everyone with a short break or a day out somewhere they will want to take part in. A sustained amount of family time can help to calm this kind of manic planning.

Stand by your parenting

I'll put this crudely. Our kids may knock about with kids who are barely being parented. Being parented can feel like a giant pain in the a***e when your friends run around unencumbered by things like bedtimes, mealtimes and rules. It can seem to them as though being parented is not the norm. This may unleash an attack on your right to parent like you've never in your life experienced. It may even cause you to question whether you are the one in the wrong.

Reassess what's important, don't waste energy sweating the small stuff, but also stand firm in your role. Our kids need parents, even if they don't think they do.

Value the good friendships
I enjoy the times that friends are in our house. I like teenagers, I enjoy our home when people visit and eat and sleepover. The good friendships our children make might not be what we ever expected but they might be all the more interesting and precious for that.

Drugs and alcohol
If you have a child who has always strained to reach for the next item or substance on the ladder of parental disapproval then you may need to fasten your seatbelt. What starts with a school rucksack full of energy drinks can evolve into a small crossover bag full of drugs.

Many of our young people experiment with drugs in a controlled, contained manner and you'll know whether your young person is likely to do it this way, or not. Either way, if you are concerned, it might be best to prepare yourself.

A need for control alongside dysregulation, impulsivity, a drive to belong to a dysfunctional peer group and a general need to piss off your parents means our children are especially vulnerable to drug-taking. Once they discover drugs, I'm told the calming effects on a traumatised and stressed-up system can feel like a blessed relief from reality. This is without doubt the case. It can also in some circumstances be a useful excuse inviting sympathy (attachment-seeking, not attention-seeking, stupid!) and dodging responsibility.

I refer to drugs but it might equally be alcohol or a mix

of both. In my vicarious experience, alcohol is a rather passé way of screwing yourself up. Perhaps there may be genetic predispositions either way, I don't know. What I do know, unfortunately, is that drugs are cheap, easy to carry around, available and are being traded on street corners and car parks and parks in every village, town and city across our fair land. Most law-abiding citizens have little idea of the prevalence of the drug trade and drug-taking and I don't often see it reported as the huge social issue I think it is. But that's as an aside.

Our young people, wearing their vulnerabilities on their sleeves, may, without realising it, find themselves at very great risk. The risk comes not only from the drugs themselves, that are, let's face it, not that well safety-tested or analysed for rogue ingredients, but also from those who sell them. The drug trade is financially very lucrative for those at the top of the pyramid selling scheme and less so for the disposable minions at the bottom. Where there is much money to be earned and intense competition to earn it there is sure to be intimidation and violence involved. This is not Tupperware. This is a dark, dangerous world that our young people can find themselves embroiled in. If only they'd study and go to college instead!

The first and most important step for us, their worried parents, is to avail ourselves of information. What drugs are on the market? What form do they come in? What are their effects? Why do young people take them? What Class are they? What is the criminal justice response to being caught in possession of them? The internet is your best bet for getting this information. I like the website www.talktofrank.com. I've used other websites when I've had specific questions such as 'what is a K-hole?' (it's really screwed up my search history). If you find yourself searching similar terms, never imagining this is where you'd end up, you really do have my greatest sympathy. It's tough going, lonely and frightening. Did preparation training cover this stuff? I don't think it did.

If you have the courage, then I'd recommend watching the BBC series Drugsland: short documentary pieces that show modern drug-dealing and exploitation including the county lines network (something else we have social media to thank for). Stacy Dooley's BBC documentary Kids Selling Drugs Online is worth watching too.

There may be a need for us to be vigilant in terms of who our young people are consorting with, whether there are signs of 'using' and whether there are unusual amounts of money flashing around, several mobile phones, streams of messages and regular 'meet-ups'. You may have to make carefully balanced decisions about involving services. The police may get involved either through choice or necessity. I've found the police to be supportive, well informed and compassionate. They work hard to avoid criminalising young people although once the eighteenth birthday bell strikes it's a different ball game. When your birthday wish for your child is that they don't criminalise themselves, get violently attacked by a drug gang, take an overdose or get trafficked across the country, it's very tough going. I write these words in my garden, the sun is out for the first time in weeks, washing is drying on the line, my cat Ron is sat at my feet and the dissonance between where I am physically and mentally is something else. Therapeutic parenting takes some of us to dark places. Despite all this I remain hopeful. Years of good parenting, stability, love and family life count for something. It's all in there, even if the adolescent brain has misplaced it for a while. Eventually we come to a place where we may trust that our beloved young person will find themselves out of the chaos and that they have the skills necessary to achieve this. While they find their way, the most important steps that we, their parents, can take is to take care of ourselves. We must be strong and whole when our young people return and we must be present and able for the rest of the family. There really is no point in sacrificing ourselves on the altar of trauma. This last part of the journey is for our young people to make, while we place ourselves just beyond the finish line, providing gentle encouragement and cooking the occasional hot meal.

It's difficult to offer more concrete advice because these situations are complicated, messy and individual. You must decide the practicalities such as whether you will allow certain substances to be stored or used on your property (we don't, it's a stake in the ground for us) or how much 'pocket money' you provide. Other than that I can only pass on what I've learned, which is perhaps obvious, unless you are in the thick of it: try not to get caught up in the chaos, it's important for you and it's important for your young person that you don't.

Going missing

I'm tempted to joke here about who is going missing here, us or them. We've all dreamt at one time or another of grabbing the car keys, driving to a far-away caravan park and disappearing. But no, I mean our dearest child going missing. You can look after yourselves.

Going missing can mean all sorts of things. It can mean the flight, of the fight/flight/freeze response, or it can mean 'sod off, I'll do what I like and you can't stop me'. It can mean more worrying things too: child sexual exploitation, drug-dealing, poor mental health. If you have a child who goes missing I think it's worth working out what you're dealing with. If it's a curfew that's not respected than you will need to respond using your therapeutic and more traditional parenting tools, with the occasional bit of detective work. If you suspect something more worrying then you are likely to need the involvement of other services.

I've had to do a fair amount of detective work and I've had to think hard about how worried I should be in different situations. Sometimes we can find ourselves experiencing boundary creep when clear and sensible boundaries are chipped away at until they no longer exist. I find it helpful to talk to someone outside of the whole trauma dramarama to get a grip on really what is acceptable and what isn't. If our kids are staying out, not coming home at night and we don't know where they are then that is cause for concern. If they become secretive about where they're going and sleeping then alarm bells should ring. This all gets tricky when they reach the age of 16 and 17 because our leverage reduces dramatically. They are nevertheless still classed as children (although not in all countries, including Scotland) and ours may have developmental delays in areas that impact on their ability to keep themselves safe, over and above the usual adolescent stuff. The term 'think toddler' will never stretch as thin as at this time. At 18, they are classed as adults and at that point, within the boundaries set by law and if they are living within the normal boundaries of family life, then they can do what they like. Many of our young people struggle with both and find themselves leaving the family home one way or another.

To avoid boundary creep and to ensure we are clear of our own stakes in the ground it is vital to set out what you expect of your young person. If they disappear all night and you don't know where they are then you must consider calling the police. I hesitate to say that you have no option other than to call the police because I know something of the complexities of all this. There is much value, however, in saying, 'If you are not home by this time and you have not made contact and I don't know where you are, I will call the police.' This sets a clear boundary. And you must follow through.

Involving the police can be a difficult thing to do the first time. I really, really get that. I have come to value the involvement of the police in our lives due to their clear-sightedness, logic and sense. Other services may become available once your young person comes on to the police radar and if there are concerns around, for example, child sexual exploitation then you need the police involved as soon as possible. They will have knowledge and intelligence that may benefit the ultimate safety of your child immensely. And as always, the earlier the intervention, the better.

Something you may have to wrestle with is how much disruption you are willing to live with. Are you OK with your young person coming home in the early hours? Do they leave the front door wide open? Do they wake everyone up? Can you sleep when you're uncertain whether they will come home? Do you have other children at home who are being disturbed too? It is OK not to accept this. It's OK to set clear boundaries and stick to them. Our young people may no longer be able to live within our boundaries, which after all would be boundaries in most other people's homes too, and the time may come when very difficult decisions have to be made.

There are occasions when our children are late home, by half an hour or an hour and we really have to think hard about whether or not that's a big deal. Let's face it, firm time-keeping isn't always a strong point and I think it's best to set flexible times when we expect them home. And they should really respond to us when we message them with a 'are you on your way home?' We get to know whether our children are losing track of time, swinging things just a bit, or out of control and unsafe.

If we have a child whose response is flight rather than fight, or is learning to, the return home can be a good moment to praise them, depending on the circumstances. They may be scared we are going to react badly and that may keep them out longer the next time. A display of not being angry, welcoming them back home and even praising them for not acting out aggressively can be just what they need.

CHAPTER 10

Who am I?

The question of identity

'Who am I? Am I my DNA or am I something different, more or even separate from it?' is a giant question we all take time to work through and, we hope, come to some understanding of and peace with. These are questions involving a unique set of circumstances and experiences and questions that each of us can ultimately only explore for ourselves. They are the loneliest of questions and yet answering them can bring the freedom and confidence to step into the world and take on successful friendships, relationships, interests and careers.

This journey into adulthood is complicated enough even for those of us who grew up surrounded by good, working examples of those with whom we share DNA, who loved and cared for us and created a world around us that was safe and secure. We stepped out into the world from a secure base, with a growing and cohesive sense of ourselves that developed alongside our independence. Of course, even those of us with the most secure of starts can struggle with identity but what our children face is mind-blowingly complex and a factor more difficult than most people ever have to contend with.

Part of our job as therapeutic parents is to face up to the

astoundingly massive questions our children have to wrestle with, to accept that this is their reality. Trying to see the world through their eyes is something we get better and better at and it's a good job, because this is when our skills really come into their own.

Am I like my birth family, or my foster or adoptive family? Do I have any choice in the matter? Do I have power and agency? Am I a bad person who doesn't deserve to live a good life? How much is inevitable? Our children are living the extremes of the nature-versus-nurture debate for real, with layers of shame, anger and confusion on top. And it is a horrible irony that those with the most painful and thorny questions to face may be least well equipped and supported to help them arrive at some answers. We hope that they will go about things carefully and with help but that's not always how our children roll. Impulsivity, difficulties in thinking out consequences, social media and the adolescent brain can propel them along at a hundred miles an hour, without a seat belt.

Looking in on it all and experiencing the shock waves can give us the overwhelming need to reassure our young people that they are good and worthy, loved and cherished and so much more than a bundle of DNA and a complex, perhaps poor start in life that they didn't deserve. We are right to want to reassure them but unless and until our loved ones have explored all the main roads, side roads, dead ends and empty houses, they are just words, even though they do bear repeating, with heart, from time to time. We may, though, find ourselves out in the cold while they try to find the way for themselves because it may just be too confusing to have us around. Again, we may have to be the human embodiments of the safe port in the storm, ready to welcome them home on their return.

In an ideal world, our children would have some high-quality, high-support, therapeutic life story work under their belts and be arriving at an integrated sense of who they are and their place in the world. I can't write with much authority on the ideal world but I will pass on the approach I've taken and what I've learned along the way.

Be secure in your relationship with your child

When we operate from a secure understanding that we are their family, however that looks, the people who raised them, nurtured them, loved them and nothing will ever change that, that security allows us to stand firm while our child explores their birth family relationships however they need to. A wish to explore birth family is not a rejection of us, even though it may feel like that for a time. Our children may struggle to keep us close while they explore. Wasn't it always the way?

Ensure nothing is off limits

If we are queasy about or unmoored by aspects of our child's past and our child detects it (which hyper-vigilantly speaking they surely will) it risks heightening feelings of shame. If we can't bear our child's identity in its fullest sense, how can they? That's not to say it's going to be easy. Doubts must, I think, be expressed in private. And don't we know that any negativity expressed by us will only set the stage for a control battle? Signs of queasiness may also cause our child to keep secrets. They may feel they are protecting us from certain truths through fear of rejection. 'Look, I can take whatever comes' is the message we want to be broadcasting. I also believe we should leave an offer on the table to facilitate, if it's safe to do so, connections with birth family, whether that's organising support services or providing transport or meeting up. As always, this offer is wrapped in support and acceptance and set in the context of our child's wishes. If they wish to reconnect, or disconnect, then that is their choice and to pretend differently is to deny their wishes. I don't have much experience of positive birth family connections but I know to be led by my child. Whether I hear 'I want to see that person' or 'I want to kill that person' I must honour it.

Be led

This may not work or even be the right approach in your family, but I've learned to be led when it comes to discussions about birth family members. It's particularly necessary, I believe, where there are siblings, each with different experiences and viewpoints. That's not to say I've avoided difficult conversations because I haven't and I've initiated many. The old tropes ('he did the best he could', 'there are probably good reasons why') didn't wash. If a child is angry about something that did or didn't happen then that can't be explained or reasoned away. Likewise, if they are exploring then as long as they are doing this relatively safely, who are we to pour cold water on that? It's also important to remember that some of our children want to understand the basics but very much see themselves as our children and cack-handed attempts to encourage them to reconnect may come across as ill considered and even rejecting. So, aside from good-quality life story work (still dislike that term by the way), this is how I've gone about things.

Be the calm port in the storm

To return to a common theme, we must endeavour to be the embodiment of the safe port in the storm. Be clear about whose chaos this is and revisit efforts to get caught up in someone else's. If we all get entangled, then we all risk going down. Someone needs to be standing tall and firm when the storm has passed over and that someone has to be you.

Give options

'If you ever want to find out more about your birth family, or meet members of your birth family just let me know. We can get that organised in a safe way that will protect everyone involved, especially you.' Saying this now and again is an important indicator that you are man or woman enough for whatever's in store. However...

Expect a mess

Going about things the organised and careful way is not, shall we say, always how our children roll. Expect things to be messy, ill considered and reactionary and you may not be disappointed.

Social media

Expect a few social media shockers along the way too. It can be like watching a car crash and that's just the car crash you know about. The first social media shocker is the worst. My only advice is breathe and try not to panic, then ring your social worker.

Fear

If there are risky and perhaps dangerous individuals who have lurked in your child's fears for years then this can be the time when they face those fears and experience additional anger and confusion. 'How could you have done that to me?' is a valid question that will open up unpleasant truths that some may not yet be ready to face. Answers may still prove unsatisfactory and there may be a sense of unfinished business and things left unsaid. Learning to sit with the mess and discomfort but not to be defined by it must, I think, be a very difficult thing to do indeed and I'm lucky that I've never had to. Again, our children may have to figure all this out at a distance from us. Let's make sure that while they are working things through, we are focusing on being strong and well. I've said it before and it's worth repeating: what is the point of it all if we all get washed away by a messy white wave of trauma?

Grief
If our children go in search of their birth families they may not discover them intact. There may be real and fantasy deaths, losses and shocks to process. It seems trite to try to express how complicated and multi-layered that might be. All we may be able to do in support is provide loving and sturdy messages, to demonstrate our unwavering presence and to show empathy. We may also have to keep in mind that grief, pain, anger and blame are bedfellows.

Happy extended families?
There is a spectrum of contact between adoptive, foster, birth family members, family friends, care workers and suchlike from none to some difficult encounters to 'hey, we're all part of the same happy family'. There is of course no 'one size fits all', how could there be? You may like and support members of your child's birth family. But some of our children were removed in truly shocking circumstances and you may need to keep a safe distance even if your child gets dangerously close. It's important to remember that you have a choice. There are fantasies everywhere you look in adoption and fostering and in therapeutic parenting generally and I think we're done with being hijacked by them.

Keeper of the information
Here's some clean, practical advice. Make a file of your child's essential information, the forms, certificates, documents. Their journey through the care system may be long and windy, they may have had many social workers and information will have

been lost or archived along the way. There may even be a war of disinformation at various points. It's best not to get involved, other than to point various individuals towards the relevant parts of the paperwork. If young people are in a position to hold their own information then be sure to keep a copy. I'd put money on it that you're the safest custodian. You will be thanked in the future for your care and consideration, especially if you include a short note, something perhaps like 'I put this together and kept it for you, lots of love'.

What do you want to be?

'What do you want to be?' is a question that still flummoxes me and it can floor our loved ones. After all, how can you know what you want to be, if you're not sure who you are? And how can you hold an ambition for the future, when you may have difficulties grasping time or trusting in something better? An ambition is a big thing and not realised in one step. Breaking down an ambition into achievable chunks also requires skills and a belief that our young people might not yet have and might need help with. We might need to carry out some of the legwork that their peers do for themselves. Working towards an ambition is the ultimate in investing now, to reap a future return. To invest in yourself, you need to believe that you're worth something.

Even where there are strong ambitions these may be mixed up with fantasies and shaped by trauma. Rescuing, saving, nurturing, feeding are themes I see cropping up with some frequency. And if a fantasy is revealed as such and gets dashed on the rocks, the resulting sense of hopelessness and loss can be overwhelming.

Unfortunately, at the point our children are still in need of a few years of catch-up time to allow knowledge, experience and maturity to settle, the education and training systems shout,

'What do you want to be?' It's a pity our children can't hold off specialising and instead explore themselves and the world for a few more years, in a structured, full-time, unpatronising, 'please get out of the house' kind of a way.

Many of our young people come into their own after a few false starts and falls into their twenties and beyond. It's a long game and all we may able to do to support them is to keep propping doors open and gently encouraging them to see what lies on the other side. Everyone has talents and possibilities and there is always hope. We may need to keep hope wrapped up safe and bring it out from time to time. 'You'd be good at that', 'I don't mind coming with you to take a look', 'There's no pressure to decide, maybe do what you think you'd enjoy for a couple of years' are all, I think, powerful messages to give.

CHAPTER 11

The Strains of Independence

When we get down to brass tacks, parenting is really about preparing our children to venture out into the world and live independently. As parents we work towards our eventual redundancy, looking forward to those golden years when we are still young enough to live life, enjoy time with our adult children and have the freedom and lack of responsibilities to do so. Or so the story goes.

A 'spiky' developmental profile and a few layers of attachment messiness and trauma can make for a particularly bumpy pathway to independence. That's not to say that 'all teenagers' don't experience some degree of bumpiness, of course many of them do, it's a massive, the massive, life transition. But it can get to the point when absolutely no one can say, with any honesty, 'well, all teenagers do that'. I write this shortly after waving the police off, again. I can't remember how many times the blue and yellows have pulled up outside our house. I'm on first name terms with one of the PCSOs (Police Community Support Officer). He's very nice. He's called Andy. I hope Andy never reads this.

Some of our teenagers are straining to get away, before they are ready to, others lack the confidence to take the strain and many are a confusing mixture of the two. I want to say I don't know what's harder, but you know, the police have just been and when you have to answer clear questions with clear answers, you realise how messed up things have become.

In an ideal world, our securely attached young people gradually migrate from the bosom of family into the bosom of established and healthy friendships. In many of our worlds, our attachment-challenged young people bounce into the open arms of transient young people and adults who are neither protective nor good role models. It's the worst of both worlds. What we can experience as parents positioned at one point of the independence triad is a very jagged, inconsistent and strained letting go. If this were a relay race, we'd have the baton grabbed from our hand before the line, then maybe even thrown back in our faces. It's a very confusing time.

When I analyse independence in our children it seems much more like the cry of 'I need control' rather than 'I need independence'. Control and independence are two different motivations and although I've come to this conclusion myself (and post-police and peak frazzled brain so I could be way off here), I think the difference lies at the heart of why attaining independence can be a great big nightmare in our families. Independence is partly driven by the need to separate from family and partly by having gained skills. I took driving lessons, learned to drive, took my test, passed (eventually), drove on my own and gathered confidence. I became an independent driver. I didn't refuse to learn, ignore all advice, grab my parent's car keys and career off into town leaving a trail of destruction behind me. That's not independence, but some of our young people confuse this kind of carry-on as independence. They may also misinterpret it as being able to do exactly what they want, when they want, with no expectation of responsibility or consequences. It's adulthood, seen through the eyes of a young child. It's an immature take on adulthood, with impaired skills around risk and consequential thinking. It's the 'spiky profile' at its most extreme. For parents it's the spiky profile at its most terrifying.

When our children are young adolescents, our job is to parent them and keep them safe and although that can be difficult enough, our responsibilities are clear and no one disagrees. We make sure they go to school, if they don't come home at night we report them missing, we make sure they eat, sleep and we try our best to keep boundaries in place. As they get older, not only do they make this a lot harder as they wrestle us for control, but society makes it harder too. Society does not generally understand or take account of the spiky profile. By the age of 16 and most certainly by 17 our children will be afforded freedom and responsibility that many of them are just not yet equipped for. This freedom may in certain circumstances run contrary to their best interests. This may be especially stark if they are running around with young people who are not being parented at all, and haven't been for many years. Basically, we become giant party-poopers, albeit giant party-poopers who are still expected to rush in when some massive heap of trouble lands. It may come to the point when you get the urge to smack yourself in the face whenever you hear someone say, 'Well, she is old enough to make these choices for herself.' It saves a lot of time and energy. It skips the bit where we patiently explain various likely outcomes, watch one of those outcomes happen, mop up after it and then diplomatically say, 'I tried to warn you.'

All this considered, it is worth stepping back and considering what is magic about independence. I have loved witnessing a visit to the park with some friends, a bus ride into town, a party, a meal out. A lot can go right during this time and we can allow ourselves some pride that we have done our bit to pass on great skills. Success during independence breeds success. And a little bumpiness may be talked through and rectified, plans can be readjusted and expectations reaffirmed. When there is growing confidence it means we can reduce our own threat detection system and relax a little when our child is out exploring the world.

I'm going to stick my neck out here and suggest that none of us escapes the strains of independence nor gets through it unscathed. And although we must of course value what is great about growing independence, how do we cope with the rest of it? Here are a few brain pickings and learnings that I have come upon.

Whose wrong is it?

Our role during the strains of independence becomes rather less clear than at any other time preceding it. It's easy, if not unavoidable, to get it wrong: either by being overly protective ('Why are you SO controlling?') or feeling the strong pull to give up and get it all over with ('Why is tea late? I'm REALLY hungry and it's YOUR FAULT'). You may find yourself saying out loud to no one in particular, 'I can't do right for doing wrong.' One of the 'go to' tools in my toolbox of hard-learnt lessons is to listen to what I say out loud and to consider how I might voice that to the young person concerned. It's no good saying to them, in exasperation, 'I can't do right for doing wrong' because they will agree with you. Far better to try something along the lines of 'I can't get this right for you'. Then you might attempt 'you asked me for X, I got you X and now you're cross with me because X isn't what you wanted'. Another way of putting this is 'when things go wrong, I get the blame'. It's far easier to blame someone close to you when things don't go as imagined than to own a mistake and work out a way of resolving it. Our kids can find both of these skills spectacularly difficult. Far easier to deflect the jab of pain and failure towards your parent.

I am terrible at this, but I work hard not to let the 'wrong' stick on me. I am often accused of being in the wrong, of buying the wrong trousers, of not laundering something well enough, of forgetting I'd agreed to something I (am pretty sure) hadn't, of stepping in to keep someone safe when they are careering towards danger. I hear the cries of 'all teenagers' but the difference is in the relentlessness, the extremes and the fallout, as I'm sure you know. We can find ourselves being ground down by being relentlessly wrong and being treated like dog crap. Clear thinking and some time away from the crapshow are the way forward. Repeat after me, 'This is not my wrong.' Do not take part in the crapshow. Do not start to believe that this is your wrong.

Needy Rejectingness (or Rejecting Neediness)

The spiky profile has a lot to answer for and one of its more irksome traits is the needy rejectingness or the rejecting neediness. I hate you, I love you, I need you, leave me alone, come here, forget it, I want you. Pull. Push. Pull. Push. Pull. Push. Screaming toddler. Semi-adult. Over and over and over. It's like being dragged by the emotional hair, up and down the stairs.

When you find yourself at the mercy of Needy Rejectingness, think carefully about how you can step out and refuse to be dragged round by the emotional hair. Think about how you can regain your power and agency. Think about being active rather than reactive. Can you get in ahead of the cycle and make a prediction out loud to shock it a bit? Also consider whether you are reverting to type and playing out your designated role of rescuer, fixer or withdrawer, reverting to your Default Super-Hero.

Our dearest do, of course, need us to sort stuff for them and be there probably more than their peers need their parents. But they detest themselves for needing us as much as they do. Needing someone's help is a sign of vulnerability and vulnerability is not a safe state to be in. For that reason, we may have to provide some essential help in ways that prevent our young people from appearing and feeling vulnerable. The Rescue by Stealth is the type of mission we may have to get very good at. Going about things cunningly. Approaching other trusted adults around them to provide some help or offer some wise counsel. Often help and advice is a sweeter dish to sup on when served up by someone who is not your annoying parent.

Pinging back after a heavy rejection may be hard to take, for us. We may still be bruised from the rejection while our beloved one is bouncing around, telling jokes and juggling with tangerines. This is the 'I can't bear the pain of rejection' dance, the Dance of the Needy Ones. Before we know it, it's our fault we aren't joining in. 'What's the matter with YOU? Why have you got a COB ON?' The fact that a mere ten minutes ago something got lobbed at you and a door was slammed into your face is of no consequence. The neediness may morph from Entertaining Needy to Clingy Needy. I particularly struggle with Clingy Needy. The best defence I have found is to say what I see:

'I think you're ashamed you treated me so badly and it hurts and you want the hurt to end as quickly as possible' (you can put your fist to your heart to demonstrate the hurt).

Leave a constructive silence.

'I feel hurt and I need time to recover.'

'It's hard for you to say sorry but that might be the best way of repairing this.'

'When you say I love you over and over I think you mean "I'm sorry and I'm scared you've disconnected from me."'

Slowing down and disrupting the cycle of Needy Rejectingness is what we're aiming for. We're also aiming to avoid becoming needy and rejecting ourselves. It can be catching.

Rebellion

Rebelling against your parents is healthy, right? Fashion choices, haircuts, piercings, tattoos, smoking, an unsuitable boyfriend or girlfriend? Most of us rebelled and our rebellions might have involved some of these aspects of growing up and gaining independence.

When I watch other young people around me rebel, it looks a bit wayward and out-of-control, but it isn't entirely. It's waywardness, done with a nod to safety. Controlled rebellion. When I watch our young people rebel, the safety catch is off. They attack our values and tastes, but they can end up picking on the wrong ones, values and tastes that society shares. Again, this is independence gone askew.

The rebellion I witness is about attacking basic human rights and expressing some pretty filthy opinions about minority groups. It seems quite common in our families. I think it's partly because our kids are good at identifying the things we hold dear and using them against us. It makes them sound cold and calculating which they are not, but that doesn't take away from the shock at hearing something utterly revolting. Rascism, sexism, homophobia, animal cruelty, religious hatred, you name it, nothing may be off-limits. 'I'm not you,' they are really saying, 'I can think for myself.'

They will not get the context and this makes them vulnerable to grooming by certain online groups. Britain's scumbag far-right parties know the value of targeting vulnerable young people online and unfortunately some of our young people will roll over in front of them and let them tickle their tummies. And what better relief from the pain of feeling yourself unworthy and bad than to look down on someone you perceive to have less power than you do and to project your self-hatred on to them. It's the human condition for real.

If you are experiencing teen rebellion of whatever flavour then I fear the stronger and more passionate your defence, the worse it will become. I have tried to maintain a strong defence of few words and confident body language. I have often failed. The real lessons have been taught by the outside world. My job has been to maintain my position and to remember that I don't have to justify myself or my values to a 16-year-old.

Here are some more strategies that I've found may ease the strains of independence.

Nurture Attack
When our child pings back to us as a result of some disastrous experience outside the home, that we may or may not have tried to warn them about, an opportunity presents itself for a Nurture Attack. We may empathise, pick up the emotional pieces and deliver a ton of nurture. Home feels a good place to be when your mum or dad takes care of you, gives you their time, brings you snacks and downloads the film you've been looking forward to seeing. These windows of opportunity are like gold dust.

Practical skills
You may by now have an inkling as to whether your loved one is going to do the leaving home bit relatively smoothly or not.

If you suspect 'or not' then now may be the time to teach as many independence skills as you can, when circumstances allow. Skills around cooking, washing up, laundry, finances, reading a timetable and filling in a form will all come in useful. If you have a window of opportunity when your child can take this kind of coaching from you, make the most of it. The window may slam shut very quickly and once it's closed, well, all I can say is, delivering a lesson on how to set the washing machine on a 40°C mixed coloureds cycle might not be top of your priority list.

Friends trump family

In the 'all or nothing' school of being an adolescent the move away from family and towards 'friends' may happen suddenly, strangely and with a few big bounces. Most parents have a bit of time to adjust to the change in pecking order. Therapeutic parents may not get much time at all. Acceptance is the only way I'm afraid: acceptance that you have become a peripheral person in their lives and that they have chosen, for now, some interesting characters to replace you with. Grieve as you need to and remember that this is probably not a permanent state of affairs. Focus on rebuilding your life. You're a damn fine person to have around and your kid will come to realise that.

A busy weekend

When everyone is exhausted from the jagged strains of independence, why not plan a fun-packed weekend? If you feel up to it, a busy weekend, especially when you can get away, keeps certain people off the streets, away from unhelpful influences and reaffirms the presence and warmth of the family unit.

The harder you pull...

Who doesn't love a game of Tug O'War in the sunshine at the village fair after a cider or two? The problem with the adolescent, slightly less fun version of this game, is it's about winning and losing and you know who the loser is here, don't you?

The harder we pull them towards us and away from trouble the harder they pull away from us. Sometimes it's best to stop pulling and play a different game instead. Just don't replace it with Whack A Mole. That really is a fool's game.

Create the home you want to live in

Have you ever walked along a street as it's getting dark, glanced into someone's lit-up house and witnessed a scene of warmth and belonging? Have you felt the urge to step inside and feel some of that warmth? Our separateness is felt all the more keenly because we are out in the cold, removed, even though we are separated by only a few metres and a brick wall.

One of the wise ones in my life advised me to create the kind of home life that our child might look in on with the same yearning. Our children have to want to belong with us. What is there, of value, to belong to if our home lives are left in carnage?

The Invisible Thread

The Invisible Thread is a useful strategy throughout our parenting tenure and it's particularly powerful during the strains of independence. The Invisible Thread is a short, thoughtful text, it's a bag of sweets, it's the offer of a lift, it's 'no strings attached'. It says, 'I'm a constant in your life'; it says, 'I love you no matter what.' It is different from 'I'm a doormat and I'll keep running around after you.' The Invisible Thread is on your terms. It's a random act of kindness and thoughtfulness. It is best delivered when we feel like delivering it but can also be faked when we have run out of steam.

Leaving home

We all hope that our loved ones will leave home when they have the skills for independence and in a planned and safe way, allowing for our support when they need it and even when they don't. We may imagine a nice flat, a shared house or a room in a college campus and many of our young people manage this transition in these ways and quite successfully.

However.

I'm going to assume that either your loved one is going at it with the drive of an adult and the skills and vulnerabilities of a much younger child or that they are so fearful of the world you wonder if they will ever leave home. That's in-y and out-y trauma for you, quite literally.

I don't have any experience of the 'not leaving the house' type of in-y, delayed transition, so you will have to rely on the expertise of message boards and Facebook groups, of which there are plenty around which offer good advice and support. What I do have is *some* experience of the crash-bang-bounce-blue light-out-y premature transition. If this is what you are seeing on the horizon or are in the throes of then, my goodness, isn't it horrific?

Many of us carry the emotional if not the physical scars from The Leaving. A burning need for control, a lurch towards friendship groups, an absolute refusal to abide by any of the usual family ways of doing things and a blindness when it comes to recognising the needs and safety of anyone else in the home can all come together to cause the most earth-shattering nuclear explosion. It may be running away, or being made homeless or being carted off by an emergency service; either way, it's not pretty and it is unfortunately extremely traumatising for everyone involved. I think we all know when family life is that unsafe that we have no option but to press the nuclear button. It may be that you have a younger child or children in the home and their safety is of grave concern. It may be that all of you are ill and exhausted from living in a soup of toxic trauma or it may be that your young person leaves of their own accord. There may be drugs or alcohol involved, dangerous associates, criminality, violence and multiple disappearances.

The Leaving isn't something that is instigated easily by any of us and indeed many of us hang on longer than we should in the valiant hope that things will improve. We may start to normalise a situation that is a very long way from normal until one day something extreme tips us over.

When our child leaves home in this way we are left with a mixture of conflicting thoughts and feelings. We may first be struck by how peaceful our home now is, that we no longer have to live on our nerves, that we can sleep through the night without worry. We may then start to realise how bad things had got and then as we start to relax a little, the descent into post-trauma might start. Post-trauma for me was a feeling of disconnectedness, complete lack of energy, staring into space. I felt as thought I'd walked out of an horrific car crash. I lapped up the silence and the silence rang in my ears. Then the worry came back. The worry wormed away for months and still does but I am learning how to live well with it running like an app in the background. More of that later.

Once the dust has settled we may reflect on how The Leaving played out and realise that it was uncannily similar to how our loved one left their birth family home. We may wonder how that could have happened and whether strong psychological currents were at play all along and whether we ever had the power to swim against them.

CHAPTER 12

Parenting from a Distance

Although we may hope and plan that our young people gradually gain a healthy independence and leave home at an appropriate age and in a managed way, many of them don't. What we should really say is that many of them can't. Services around them and us don't take enough account of the 'can't'. Those of us left in shock may be reflecting on the inevitability of the manner of The Leaving because for many it has been a case of 'when' and not 'if'. There is much to be learned about effective ways of supporting those taking care of adolescents with enormous amounts of unresolved trauma so that the chances of the catastrophic leaving home and its impact if it does happen are reduced. It's more cost-effective, safer and much less traumatic if young people and their families are supported at home, with regular breaks and a carefully managed transition out of home than for services to step in once crisis point has been reached. If you are parenting from a distance or are close to it, then you won't need me to spell any of this out.

The crisis point

Your young person may not leave home as the result of a crisis, but if they do then it might pan out something like this.

There are many ways the crisis point may be reached and many ways of describing it. Dysregulation, a lack of cause-and-effect thinking, increased risk-taking, a refusal to abide by boundaries and an increase in controlling behaviours are all disinfected ways of capturing what living with a young person who is spiralling out of control might look like. Those of us on the receiving end of this battering of family life may describe things a little less cleanly. The crisis point may be reached after a prolonged period of unbearable emotional and psychological torture. The fact that our young people aren't choosing to be dangerous, selfish a***holes to live with, doesn't take away from the fact that this is the fact of the matter.

You may want to inform me that all teenagers can be dangerous, selfish a***holes, so here we go.

Your young person does not work or engage in any education at all and so they spend large amounts of time at home. If you leave them alone in the home then there is a high risk they will steal valuable items so you either organise your home like a secure institution or you stay home with them. They are also not safe around their siblings, so you have to supervise them at all times. You probably won't even be able to hang the washing out or take a phone call. When they don't get exactly what they want, when they want it, like for example fifty quid, or a Pot Noodle, they become abusive, swearing very loudly in your face, calling you a whore, bitch or whatever and will follow you if you walk away. There will be graphic physical threats and threats to your home and its contents. You hear uncommonly loud destructive noises often and live on your nerves. You find yourself in situations where you have to calculate where the younger children are in your house, where the telephone is, the route you could take out of the house and where you will head for. There will be times when it is not outside the realm of possibility that someone will end up dead, from a punch to the face, a strangling, or a blow from a heavy object. Sometimes you wish it would just happen so it would all be over. Your young person will go out without warning and refuse to tell you where they are going. They will tell you lots of things, but never ask you anything. They will tell you they are staying with someone for two nights, then text you to inform you the two nights will probably turn into four. You tell them you will report them missing if they don't come home that night. They regularly come home looking very tired and their eyes look strange. They sleep for an entire day, take all the food from the cupboards and go out again. Your young person may be 15, 16 or 17. They control the home, its emotional temperature and what other family members can and cannot do, down to when they can shower and when they can sleep. No one feels safe. Younger children and adults develop serious mental health concerns.

I think we can all agree that this isn't normal family life with an average teenager. This is life with a seriously traumatised young person, who is seriously traumatising those around them.

The crisis point may be a disappearance, or moving in with someone else, or may involve a sudden rupture such as the involvement of the police. Either way, it can feel like a relief and a tragedy all at the same time. If you find yourselves parenting from a distance or on the verge, then I will walk you through what I have learned both from my own experience and those around me. If you are on the verge then I will offer you this – many therapeutic parents I know reflect that they hung on way longer than they should have and that the hanging on was done out of fear for the future and a sense of failure. The hanging on ultimately only delayed the inevitable and exposed everyone to more, unnecessary, trauma.

The aftermath – you

In the aftermath, set amongst the emotional ruins, is a profoundly upsetting and conflicting time. There is a great sense of relief that the chaos has moved out and a great sense of guilt, anxiety and fear for the future. Many of us are actually in a state of post-trauma, secondary trauma or whatever you want to call it, at this point. Personally I wouldn't call it secondary trauma. There's nothing secondary about feeling physically unsafe in your own home and then having your family rupture apart.

Despite what might be playing out away from home, your first priority is your and your family's recovery. Think about your safety as this will calm anxieties and particularly think about whether you need to change locks, PINs and access codes. Cancel extraneous appointments and commitments. Sleep. Eat well. Get outdoors. Breathe fresh air. Sleep some more. This is the time for psychological first aid.

The aftermath – your young person

The aftermath that your young person and the services around them experience in these early weeks of The Leaving are likely to be chaotic, dismembered and wild. You may hope that everyone comes to their senses and does the right thing, and that may happen, but don't bank on it. What plays out might be raging attachment dysfunction, raging trauma, raging chaos, the like of which you had never anticipated. It will demonstrate what you've been managing all these years and what you had mainly been parenting successfully. There may be a period of adjustment as services recognise the full extent of the problem.

Parenting from a distance in the short term

It may be difficult to get into any kind of routine or way of doing things in the early weeks and months of parenting from a distance; however, there are a few specks of parenting we may be able to deliver that will maintain the invisible thread of 'we still care about you' and 'our relationship will endure'.

Keep in contact using texts or messages, especially when face-to-face contact isn't possible. Beware of getting tied up in control battles, so step back if you need to. Some of our children respond well to written correspondence; there is perhaps something about handwriting rather than text that conveys warmth, meaning and connection (and let's face it, everyone likes receiving post). There may be mileage in providing family photographs, especially of happier times. I am a fan of the drip effect especially when we suspect we must settle in for the long game.

Providing bags of food and toiletries can send a strong message of nurture as can carrying out laundry. When this is possible, and it isn't always, familiar items can demonstrate your thoughtfulness. Again, this is the golden thread but in a supermarket carrier bag. Taste and smell are routes into the brain that we should use to our advantage.

Meeting up after The Leaving can be very difficult for everyone and not all members of the family may be ready to do this at the same time. Emotions will still be high and feelings raw. It is my view that it has to happen when we are ready. If you meet your young person again and it leaves you feeling sick (re-traumatised) and seriously hampers your recovery it's worth thinking very carefully about whether it's the right time. It's also important to consider where you meet. Doing it in the family home may be too much and may send everyone back into the dynamic that existed when you were all together. Somewhere neutral may work best. If this is what works for you and yours then please do not feel guilty and do not get pressured by those who don't understand the dynamics of the trauma into opening up your home. Home must become a sanctuary for those of you left living there.

Advocating

In order to advocate effectively you must be taking good care of yourself. It is likely that in the early days, and quite possibly for a long time to come after The Leaving, you will be struggling with the after-shocks of trauma. Accept this and don't blame yourself. You are doing the very best you can.

If you can, try to guard against coming across as ranty (aka traumatised), angry (traumatised), rambly (traumatised) or cold (traumatised). Set out what you want to achieve and work out who your supporters are. Before meetings, put on your Strategic Thinking Hat and make some notes. What are the 'nice to haves' and the 'essentials'? What do you need to know? What are the options (if there are any)? You are likely to have a steep learning curve because, let's face it, which of us understands the ins and outs of local services for vulnerable young people, benefits and suchlike? It's OK not to know this stuff and to ask questions.

Try to hang on to the fact that you know your young person better than anyone else. This fact will become plainer and plainer as the weeks and months unfold. It can become frustrating when you can predict certain outcomes, warn of them, and then have to witness them taking place. That's the way it is, unfortunately. There may be a period when our young person controls those around them in order to get their needs met, without making any emotional investment or commitments. You may hear 'she's doing really well' and you will have to bite your tongue or risk coming across as the worst of the party-poopers. Narratives about what a terrible parent you were may also begin to creep out. This is because the shame associated with what's happened will be too much to bear. It's impossible for our young people to take responsibility when they can't take the shame. The only other course is to blame others. It can be difficult to protect ourselves emotionally from this blame but please do try not to see it as your bad, don't own it and don't feel you have to justify yourself. It is nevertheless painful and can feel like a kick in the teeth. Times can get treacherous when professionals begin to believe the narrative of the young person over yours and over bloody obvious reality. Be clear and stand proud. You have stuck with this young person through thick and thin, when no one else was around. You did an incredible job for them. It won't have been perfect because there is no such thing. Those that wish to point out the imperfections may be those who have never had to do it themselves.

Work for your young person but at the same time stick with the mantra that you have done everything you can. This train is racing along the tracks and sometimes there is very little we can do to change the outcome. It's our old friend acceptance again, in crueller times.

Rebuilding family life

Once our children have left home and it is pretty clear they are not going to return any time soon, we will realise that family life will never be the same again. It's like a really messed-up version of Empty Nest Syndrome. At this point we can either flail around in the wreckage or we can rebuild. Rebuilding does not mean that we no longer care or that our young person is no longer a very important part of our family. Everyone deserves a safe and fulfilling family life and that includes you and the family members who remain living in the family home.

My empty nest was brutal and sudden and happened alongside heading for a big birthday, sweating through the peri-menopause and losing a friend to cancer. It all combined to make a painful transition. The loss and grief were overwhelming and complicated. I was exhausted. And I was angry. I felt as though I'd been used to meet needs and then discarded when I was no longer of use. I could put up a spirited argument that this isn't the case but there is some truth in it.

I slowly came to realise that this was a new chapter in my life and, like all new chapters, where there is loss there may also be gain. This new chapter meant having the headspace to better parent and support our younger child through some important times and establishing new routines and activities that we enjoyed and which suited us. The peace, predictability and freedom were and are something to be valued. I had the headspace to design a better, more fulfilling future for myself now that I was no longer being dragged around by trauma. I have more time for hobbies, friends and trips away. After the post-trauma cloud had passed and the new normal became the normal, I kind of woke up. Putting all worries and inevitabilities aside, it can be a time for positive change.

Positive change is not a selfish act. When we are stuck in the mud of past trauma we can become uninteresting and tedious to be around. I think it's positive for our young people to be surprised by us and to experience changes in us. In time this shifts our relationship and we may find ways of providing the required practical and emotional support whilst maintaining our own wellbeing. Parenting from a distance is a new chapter in our therapeutic parenting lives and one that can be very different from that of our peers.

CHAPTER 13

Toolbox of Techniques

I'm going to throw a load of bite-sized techniques at you now. Most of these have been referred to already, but I like a listy list as a quick reference when my brain is blown. Clearly, this list is not exhaustive and the aim is that you get to add your own. Go freestyle.

Smile for the camera

Record the good times. Sometimes we all need a reminder that we had good times. You may need reminding of the enormously marvellous job you are doing. The holidays you went on, the bacon rolls you ate, the dinners you shared, the places you visited – you did all that and it's all in the memory banks. You're amazing.

Keep a record

Keeping notes of events and photographs of broken stuff and damage is a less enjoyable enterprise but can be invaluable when seeking out support. Our trauma-soaked brains are not great at remembering things. Particularly useful if some around us are making out things are not as difficult as they really are. A reality check.

Friday sweets

If you're familiar with my work you'll know about Friday sweets. These are a fun family ritual that takes place no matter what. It's Friday, I bought you some sweets. It doesn't have to be a Friday thing or a sweet thing. Must be unconditional and the same day every week.

Random acts of kindness

An obvious strategy but can get lost in the noise. Dish out a dollop of kindness even if times are hard, especially if times are hard. RAKs can change the mood music and unstick our little argumentative brains.

Droplet of praise

We know our children can't take a great big marshmallow of praise but it's still important to praise, just give it in droplets. You look nice. Those jeans suit you. You spoke to that lady kindly. That way it's not overwhelming and doesn't conflict with how they might experience themselves.

Repair the bridge, but not too quickly

When we have become disconnected from our youngest children, we rightly go in for a quick repair. Our older kids probably still need us to start the bridge repair but a repair carried out too quickly may avoid them having to sit with the pain of disconnection. We don't want them to be in pain, of course we don't, but a vital part of grown-up relationships is about learning when we have hurt or offended someone and mastering the skills to make amends. As they get older I think we should consider not rushing the repair, starting the repair, then handing the tools over to them more often. We all learn vital lessons through being able to sit with a bit of pain.

Sit in the silence

No one likes an awkward silence; however, awkward silences can chop off an argument, give us all time to think and regulate and time to let things sink in. Get comfortable with the silence. Sometimes the art of good therapeutic parenting is about doing nothing.

Don't take the bait

An argument is seldom about the thing that is being argued over. If our children have learned to do relationships messily, loudly and dramatically then we may find they are controlling the temperature of the family home. It takes two to tango though. Be wary of grabbing the bait and being reeled in to a fight to death over, I don't know, biscuits or laundry liquid.

Forgive yourself if you take the bait

Come on, we've all done it.

What did you just say?

The things we find ourselves saying out loud when we're alone in the house or pacing around the garden can be just what we need to hear. 'I have no voice,' I heard myself say as I stomped around the field flooded with anger. Suddenly it made sense. I was treading on egg shells all the time, so much that I stopped talking. It helped me identify the problem and regroup.

Take a moment

Get practised at buying yourself time. You don't need to respond to a request or react to a situation immediately, even if your teen is pressing. 'I'll think about it.' 'That's not what I was expecting. I need time to mull that over.' Be prepared to use an additional delay tactic, something like 'if you won't wait then the answer will be no'. We are aiming to make difficult decisions when our brains our working, not being bounced into a decision we may live to regret.

The clean rebuke

When a clear boundary has been breached, I think it's best to say so, cleanly and with a bit of animation. 'That was wrong' is better than 'you've really hurt me, you've hurt your mum, you've upset the cat, the neighbours...' 'That was wrong' followed with a 'and it needs to be put right' can open the door to a consequential-type of repair.

Logical consequences

Therapeutic parenting sometimes gets misinterpreted as 'no consequences, anything goes' parenting and it's not that at all. Our job is to prepare our young people for the real world to the best of their and our abilities and the real world is littered with consequences. I favour a logical and considered consequence that bears a direct relationship to whatever it was that went wrong. The purpose of a consequence is to give the opportunity to learn something, not to cause our young people to hate us. If a young person goes into town for a few hours with their friends and gets into a heap of trouble, then they don't get to do that for a while (on that evidence they are perhaps not ready for that amount of freedom anyway) and the next time they get to go out for an hour, or you go with them. You know the drill.

Respecting your own needs

That elaborate plan that involves you driving around the county, collecting, dropping off, at times that don't suit, when you're already tired from some shenanigans or other the night before. It's all right to say 'no' to something you can't cope with. Worried that saying 'no' could result in your house being smashed about? Have a think about what that really says about the power dynamics at play. And perhaps time your 'no' carefully.

Prevent failure

If our child can't see a wallet without having to go through it then we don't leave the wallet out. If they can't pass through the kitchen without helping themselves to the ten-pack of crisps, then we don't buy the ten-pack of crisps, or we keep it somewhere else. If our child gets up to no good when they are left in the house on their own, we don't leave them in the house on their own. This is a lot to do with thinking about developmental age and ability and it can stop us all being angry and triggered all of the time.

I'm really angry

'I'm really angry and I'm going to walk away, calm down and deal with this later', even said in a loud voice, is way better than stepping into a fight, all guns blazing. Practising this approach, saying it to yourself so it is easy to grab for during a potential crisis, will make you a pro at stepping away from and not into a fight and modelling good anger management skills.

I'm sorry

I know not everyone agrees with me here, but when we've lost our s**t, I think it's best to apologise. 'I shouldn't have screamed like that, I should have walked away and I'm sorry.' Again, we are modelling a good response to a bad situation. We may even be saying in a coded way 'when you lose your s**t, kid, you need to copy me and apologise'.

Forgive yourself

There's no easy way of putting this, our kids can be absolutely infuriating. When they have driven us to the edge and screamed in our faces and we lose our s**t, hell, we're only human. I would challenge anyone to remain calm all of the time under the circumstances. If you lose your s**t, apologise, forgive yourself, eat a couple of chocolate Hobnobs and move on.

It's OK to shout, sometimes

Again, not a popular view but in my world, raising my voice in a (semi)controlled way sometimes does the trick. It can shock the collective system and cause a gobby young person to stop in their tracks. I believe it's called Match Effect. I like to call it 'don't f**k with me'.

Withdraw

Stepping back for a few hours or a day or maybe even longer can send as strong a message as any that you've had enough. 'I need a break.' Everyone has time to calm down and reflect and break the cycle. When things are really dire and no one can see the wood for the trees consider taking a long weekend and leave behind a well-considered letter. This is what's happening, this is how it makes me feel, this is how we can all do our bit to make things better, I'm looking forward to seeing you.

Go easy on the big threats.

In my humblest, the 'call the police' defence should be used extremely rarely and only when absolutely necessary. Likewise, heavy catastrophising such as 'you'll end up in prison'. Ouch.

Whose s**t is this?

Is this your s**t or someone else's? In messy psychological situations step back and ask yourself this question. Do not get covered in it.

Micro-nurture delivery service

A quick in and out with a hot drink, some nice toiletries, a written note or even just a 'hi there, how are you doing?' may be all our teenagers can take from us at times. Little and often.

Say 'yes'

Ever find yourself saying 'no' to something before you've even thought about the question? When we live in what feels like a war zone our brains get used to saying 'no'. Can I meet my friend after school? No. Can I have a bag of crisps? No. We lose perspective, we get rigid and we err on the side of conflict when we are stressed. Take some time out and reset your response to err on the side of a considered 'yes'.

Wash that bedding

Wash your loved one's bedding in beautiful-smelling laundry liquid. Do this when they are living in chaos. Do this when you can barely get into their bedroom. Do this when they hate you. Do this when they love you. Clean bedding communicates comfort and nurture through smell, touch and silence.

Chess, not the musical

When we all fall into old patterns, for example you have to mention something that needs doing, or not doing and you know the reaction isn't going to be pretty and everyone will end up shouting at each other, consider plotting your moves in advance. 'I'm going to ask you something in a moment and I'm pretty sure you're going to want to shout at me, so I'm just warning you that I'm going to ask you and walk away so you have chance to consider it before reacting.'

Don't sweat the small stuff

This is a favourite of mine and one I need to frequently remind myself of. The adolescent years can bring about a wholesale re-evaluation of what is and isn't important. I've had to overlook things that in other homes would be a really big deal. It's all relative.

CHAPTER 14

Getting Serious About Self-Care

Raising our adolescent children is psychologically complex, emotionally demanding and can at times drive us to the edge of f***ing insanity. My love for my children is threaded through every fibre of me, but that doesn't mean I haven't been taken to some dark places that I sometimes doubted I would escape from. Early life trauma is way, way more powerful than it's given credit for. When we say that trauma can control the emotional temperature in the home that makes it sound like we could just step outside for a breath of fresh air and find our own temperature, but it is nothing like as easy. When I don't take good enough care of myself, trauma stalks me like a malevolent shadow. It infects my thoughts, my body, my heart, my stomach, the way I react to situations, my demeanour, my hopes and my fears. I have been in so many situations I am not equipped for, often day after day after day, with barely time for recovery in between. It's like I downloaded a game and instead of starting at difficulty level 1, I got bounced into difficulty level 9, I have no special weapons or powers and I can't just die and go back to the start. As I write this, I'm recovering from an experience I can barely put into words. It was frightening, confusing and unpredictable in ways that

I have never known before. Without going into detail, I'll say that as Mr D and I drove home from having our brains blown apart, having kept ourselves together and made a pretty good account of ourselves given the circumstances, we descended into that special kind of numbness that follows trauma. It's the kind of numbness that leaves you staring into space and feeling as though you are underwater. Then despite extreme exhaustion, you lie awake most of the night, the night after that and the night after that while your brain replays everything that happened in a jumbled and crazy way. Gradually you return to yourself, you notice your environment, the weather, you hear a bird sing and then the sadness or worry or whatever it is breaks over you in a wave and threatens to wash you away.

Our adult brains are equipped for predictability, some learning and the occasional way-out-there experience. They are not that great at sustained high-octane, nonsensical, bizarre, illogical, frightening times. Instead of happily going along, operating on a couple of apps, it needs to have all its apps open at once and Bluetooth and location services on. I know we're not meant to compare brains to computers (or phones) but the analogy works well for me. Basically, what I'm trying to say is no wonder we're exhausted.

Aside from living a high-energy life, there is the stress. Again, a shot of stress now and again isn't harmful and helps motivate us to stay safe and to shift out of our comfort zones now and again. Living in a hot pool of stress is, however, not great for our health. When I say not great, I mean terrible. If you live in a pool of hot stress you will know what it's doing to you and perhaps you worry about its effects that I'm guessing only makes matters worse. I spent some time experiencing such extreme stress that I thought either my heart was going to explode or I was going to suffocate. It was scary and a wake-up call.

Even without the way-out-there stress-inducing situations, everyday therapeutic parenting is about suppressing our natural parenting instincts, zipping our gobs shut and thinking through and carrying out a strategy, then thinking on our feet if things don't go to plan. It's preparing ourselves for meetings, talking to professionals, fielding complaints, trying to work out if there is a holiday you can all bear to go on, a meal everyone will eat, it's sucking up the small stuff that in a normal household would be big stuff. It's demanding on so many levels. And it's demanding for longer than you think it will be. Do you remember thinking your load would have lightened when your kids reached 14, 16, 18? We are on a long old road, my friends, and we're no good to anyone if we keel over. What's more, therapeutic parenting isn't about thrashing ourselves to death. No, the idea is that we move on from being high-octane therapeutic parents to live fulfilling lives of our own. That's rather difficult if your heart has exploded.

For all of the reasons I've set out, you need to take very good care of yourself. Have I convinced you yet?

What is self-care?

Self-care is a serious business. It is as essential as filling your car up with petrol, replacing its worn-out tyres and getting it serviced. It is not what the magazines refer to as 'me time'. It is not a self-satisfied bubble bath. It is not slipper socks. It is not a liver cleanse. It is not 45 minutes in the dental hygienist's chair (although I admit to quite enjoying that). Self-care is personal and may involve some of these kinds of things, if they float your boat. It is also a practice that we must develop and live by if we are to have a chance of getting through unscathed.

Live well

We all lurch into the outstretched arms of sugar, fat, alcohol and the sofa when we are super-stressed and there's nothing wrong with that. However, when those indulgences become the norm rather than the exception, our ability to cope with everyday life is compromised. My friends, we are athletes, parentally speaking, and that's how we must treat our bodies. Eat well, most of the time, get some exercise, get sufficient sleep to give your body its best opportunity of supplying you with the energy and psychological and physical health that you need.

Be the guardian of your time and energy

Energy is about basic maths. Try to take more out than you have in the tank and you will crash land. Get fussy about what you commit to and get self-ish. Stop getting guilt-tripped into doing things you don't really want to do. And remember, recharging your tank when it's empty is more difficult than when it has a bit left in it. (That bit's not maths.)

Be your own best friend

What would your best friend tell you to do? Wash the kitchen floor on the only free morning you have this week? No, they wouldn't. Be kind to yourself.

Trade up

Even if you are low in the funds department, trade up in something that you love, like the coffee you drink, or the shampoo you use. I buy myself a good loose tea and I brew it in a green teapot with a built-in strainer. The ritual and the superior taste brightens up the c***piest day.

Experiment with not worrying

The big downer about worrying is it doesn't change a thing, it just makes you feel bad. Say to yourself, perhaps if you're going somewhere nice, that for the time you are out you will switch off the worry. Give yourself permission. Let it go.

Can I change this?

That thing you're all in a knot about, can you change it, realistically? If not, let it go.

Reduce the negative

If you feel your mood slipping during a period of relentlessness, take care over the media you consume. The news, social media, depressing dramas, violent films may be best avoided. Ask yourself, will watching or reading this make me feel (a) better, or (b) worse? If the answer is (b) then consider whether you can afford to be dragged down. The same goes for friends and acquaintances. If someone makes you feel worse, don't spend precious time with them. Grow the relationships that feed your soul.

Accentuate the positive

Fill your down time with whatever makes you feel better. Laugh, sing, dance and the world will seem a better place. Music in particular can transport us to a good place by stealth. Develop a 'feel good' playlist.

Time to digest

When our poor brains are served up a giant psychological meal of drama, they need time to digest it, to make sense and work out what on earth can be done, if anything. Without digestion time, the next big meal lands on top of the undigested one and so on and so on until our brains are constipated with drama and bafflement. I think our bodies and our brains need to work through this heavy psychological food and to help the digestion process I walk or mess around in the garden. While I'm, say, striding across the fields, things fall into place, I get ideas, I see through the fog. When I'm done I often feel lighter, like I've done a giant psychological poo.

Deal with the rage

Let's face it, even the most mild-mannered of us can be driven into a screaming ball of molten rage from time to time. That rage HAS to be processed and in my experience that means working it through physically. Dig, chop, run, pedal and expel that rage. Otherwise that rage turns into horrible chemicals that hang around our systems and make us ill.

Talk about it

We all need someone we can share our troubles with. Make sure that person is sensible and isn't prone to dishing out irritating advice. In an ideal world we'd all be having trauma-informed psychological support that would act like clinical supervision. It would allow us to decompress, talk through strategies and reflect. The fact that we don't get that is insane.

Choose your support

In reality we have limited ability to choose our professional support; however, it still stands that unsupportive support isn't support, it's just another burden. I have good support right now, which means that I don't have to explain myself or explain why unworkable suggestions are unworkable. If you are struggling against support that is either misinformed or lacking in empathy or leaves you feeling exposed and blamed then I have written a short section at the end of the book for those supporting adoptive families.

Use your tools efficiently

Hacking away at trauma with the wrong end of a spade will tire you out and break your spade. Pick the right tool for the job, employ it efficiently and take regular breaks.

Whose trauma is this?

Take great care not to own trauma that isn't yours. Trauma is extremely infectious. Self-care and knowledge is your defence. If you find yourself behaving in traumatised ways, acknowledge, resolve to increase self-care and remember that nothing lasts forever.

Overwhelm

Overwhelm calls for desperate measures. Cancel what doesn't have to be done, buy ready meals, use all the time-saving gadgets you need to, call in support and if you can, take a break, get away for a few days. I know you're going to tell me this is impossible. I'm going to tell you that you risk harming yourself and your loved ones if you do not build in a break. We get good at constructing reasons why we can't: our kids won't cope, there's no one to help out, but sometimes this is our resistance speaking.

Other infectiousness

Chaos, rigid thinking, anxiety, all of these things are infectious. Create an 'air gap' between you and whatever is threatening to stick to you. Places of calm and minimalism in the house can act as a buffer.

Look after each other

Protect your relationships and be aware of the ways in which trauma may try to come between you and set you one against the other. Even without the wily ways of trauma, the stress alone can chip away, creating division and bad feelings. When we feel hurt we often reach for blame and our partners can get the brunt. Be on the same page when it comes to your understanding of trauma and the kind of parenting your children need. Think of yourselves as a strong team.

The you-ness of you

We ditch our dreams, reassess our values, shed friends and try our hardest to be therapeutic even when it goes against the grain. But is there a limit to the cutting away and casting aside?

Yes. Yes, there is.

Despite everything, you have loved, fought, wept, laughed and continued to stride out into the world because of the you-ness of you, not the someone-ness of someone else. It's the you-ness of you that brings into your family what no one else could: your interests, humour, funny quirks, your tastes, your interests, your passions. These are unique qualities that no one can teach and they're quite possibly qualities that stood out during your preparation training and that led to you being matched with your children.

It can feel as though therapeutic parenting is about suppression of self. Sure, we are all learning how to be the parents our children need us to be and that involves a lot of compromise but it mustn't mean ditching the you-ness of you and the me-ness of me.

Quite apart from the importance of preserving and developing our you- and me-ness for our own wellbeing it's important for our children too. There may come a time when parenting our adolescent children is about being rather than doing. We need to remember know how to be, authentically and with substance.

Sometimes our children benefit from looking in on family life as an observer and not a protagonist. There may be prolonged times when this is the only option for them and for us. If they come to our window and peer inside, what is it better that they see? A knacker's yard of the broken and empty shells of their loved ones, or a vibrant home of individuality, surprise, delight and interest? We want them to reach out a hand and knock on the door. 'I'd like to come back in,' is what we'd like them to think, even if they can't say it. And we need to be in a position to open the door and welcome them back in.

And if therapeutic parenting leaves us broken, then really, what is the point of it all? It's not selfish to protect the you-ness of you, it's an act of generosity for you and your family.

Don't get trapped by Therapeutic Parenting

If we're not careful, Therapeutic Parenting (as opposed to therapeutic parenting) tells us an awful lot about what we cannot say and do and feeds us ways of behaving that feel inauthentic. We worry about wondering off the designated route for fear of going wrong so we wind up sounding like an emotionless thera-bot, with a bad American accent. Our kids are highly skilled at detecting any inauthenticity so will be on to us straight away. We take on the parts of therapeutic parenting that work in our families but we mustn't let it invade us. Keep it real. Also beware of sacrificing everything on the altar of keeping shame to a minimum. How often do we find ourselves thinking, 'I can't say that – it would cause too much shame'? Sometimes straight talking is what everyone needs.

Save some for later

I hate to break this to you, but at some point your role as a parent will diminish. Make sure you have nurtured enough of yourself so there is something left, something that is not about adoption, fostering, education plans, care plans, children. Not only should we be imagining the relationships we want to have with our children when they are, say, 25 and working towards that, we should consider what we want our lives to be like when our children are 25. I'm a fine one to talk, by the way.

CHAPTER 15

Being an Effective Advocate

By now you will have been advocating for your child for some time so I don't want to patronise you. I've set out here what I have learned and the pitfalls I have stumbled into and around in an effort to give you a heads up through these adolescent years, when our advocacy role evolves. Even though advocacy looks like just being an average parent and fighting for your cubs, it takes particular skills and strategies to maximise the chances that the best possible support and understanding is achieved. This sometimes has to happen when our loved ones lack the ability to advocate for themselves and even make themselves extremely difficult to advocate for. It has to happen when we love them and when we feel like suffocating them in their beds. It's about the long game. It's about strategy with some emotion, not the other way around.

Am I leaking trauma?

As we know, trauma is highly infectious. If we live in a household full of trauma we may take on traumatised ways of doing things. We may become shouty, demanding and long-winded or withdrawn and hopeless. An experienced professional should be skilled at spotting parent trauma but if they are not, they may assume we are obnoxious, crazy people.

What I'm going to advise you is really obvious, so don't shout at me.[1] Get a truckload of self-care in before you engage in any act of advocacy, with particular focus on regulation. Go for a walk. Talk to a good friend. Get your head together. Shut whatever trauma is bubbling inside you in the under-the-stair cupboard with the other c**p for the time it takes you to make that call or attend that meeting. Then consider telling the professionals you speak with that you are struggling and explain that in as clear and stable way as you can, by email if necessary: 'I am not at my best so you'll have to excuse me.'

The same goes for those whose trauma causes them to come over as cold and statue-like and who get accused of being emotionless and uncaring. Those poor children who have to live with such an icy parent, no wonder they are messed up. Not quite the full picture, is it?

Beware of verbosity

The person or people who are tasked with supporting us and/or our child will quite probably be time-poor and work-stressed. Our job as Super Advocate is to get to the top of their to-do list and that partly depends on making their lives as easy as possible. When they get back to their desks after a bathroom break and find 75 new emails to wade through, which ones are they going to deal with first? The 2000-word rambling rants or the succinct and to the point 250-word requests?

When we are stressed up to our eyeballs, even the naturally calmest of us can tend towards verbosity, due to the sheer incomprehensibility of one's life, the lack of power

---

[1] I'm way over being shouted at and may not respond as expected.

and the ADHD-ish effects of vicarious trauma. It's perfectly understandable and it has to be tackled with the help of understanding professionals, but it is not advocacy.

Take some time to think about whether your approach is about getting support for yourself or advocating on behalf of your child. These may be different things. If you are acting as an advocate, then make fulfilling the need of your child as easy and as pleasant as possible for the person on the receiving end. That is not to say that sometimes we may need to up the ante.

Upping the ante

When a situation has dragged on or is not being dealt with reasonably then the ante may well need to be upped. This is probably a personal thing, but I prefer to up it carefully and respectfully. I make it clear I am escalating things in the best interests of my family and that it is not personal. I avoid blame talk and talk that will get people's backs up. It's useful to be mindful that many of us are playing the long game and that going into attack mode isn't going to smooth the bureaucratic wheels and may make us the hot potato that no one wants to deal with in the future.

I'm also not a fan of escalating things too quickly. Writing to our MPs before anyone has had a chance to resolve whatever the problem is can just create more work and gets people's backs up. What I am not saying is that we don't sometimes have to escalate things right to the top. Do this when you feel you have no other choice. You probably only have one shot at this.

Keep a record

It's getting boring, I know, but please, please keep a written record of all significant events and if necessary send regular, succinct updates to your social worker. This is particularly important if you experience a lot of violence in your home and if you fear false allegations as it demonstrates you are giving everyone adequate warning and keeping everyone informed. Then if things really do go pear-shaped, you have been open and honest and covered the bases.

Know your supporters

Know your supporters and forge alliances within school, social services, extended family and other networks.

Sleep on it

Back to emails again. If I have struggled over an article all day, I will stop myself pressing 'send' even if I am desperate to get it away. The following morning it's like I possess some magic powers of editorial insight. I can spot all the problems with it; the repetition, the parts that come over too strong or not strong enough. I have learned to do this with communications to school and social services too, particularly if I've written them fuelled with a kind of 'right! I'm going to write a very strongly worded email about that!' macho energy. I have avoided sending some real stinkers by sleeping on them.

Provide succinct resources

Sharing short articles and films that get the message across without requiring a heavy investment in time will be much more effective than sliding a pile of books across a meeting room table.

Continuing education

Keep yourself informed by going to events when you can and keeping an eye on social and other media. This will develop your confidence as well as your knowledge and skills. Confidence is a big part of the key to good advocacy.

You are the expert

Do not talk down your importance. You are the most valuable person and resource in your child's life and you know them way better than anyone else. When you are preparing and attending a meeting, try to think of yourself a little bit like a professional.

There may not be an answer

I'm going to stick my neck out here: the field of mental health with regard to early adverse experiences is in its infancy. Little of real substance is known about what is effective and what recovery might look like. I suspect we will look back in horror at how early life trauma is perceived and treated right now. We're closer to the nightmare asylums of the past than we think we are and you've just got to look at youth offending and our prison population if you don't believe me. For this reason, holding out, exhausting ourselves for a magic intervention, that one solution to all the scary problems, may be fruitless. I don't mean we should give up all hope, I just mean don't die on a hill for something that might not exist. That's something that ten years ago I never thought I'd be saying. What I am certain of though is the power of good relationships.

The least c**p option

When faced with a seemingly impossible set of choices, after being crippled with bafflement for a bit, I then like to ask myself, 'What is the least c**p option?'. This is obviously not a meme that'll ever be peddled around social media in a tasteful font across a picture of a soaring bird, I accept, but sometimes, there just is no perfect solution. And there's another meme. I might create my own collection.

Who exactly is telling the truth here?

Your child comes home from school and before they are even across the threshold of the house they are spewing out a detailed account of a terrible wrong that was dealt them by another child or, even worse, a teacher! You are horrified, of course you are.

However.

Before you come over all lioness about this, take a moment to consider whether you might not be in possession of the whole story. Yes, I know, it's a shocker, but sometimes children don't tell the truth.

Who amongst us hasn't put on our fighting pants and engaged in combat only to find out that there are some giant holes in the story? I'll put my hand up to that one. It's embarrassing to have to take off your fighting pants in public.

The newsflash is: in seeking to get attention (attachment), to create drama, to stir up emotions and to prop up feelings of victimhood and bring about the rescue our children can tell an utterly convincing story. They may even believe it themselves as it might help to explain how they experienced a situation, not how it actually played out.

If we fall into these traps, and many of us do, then we just have to repair and forgive ourselves and put it down to experience. What these events should necessitate is a strengthening of the team around the child, with you at the top table. Information-sharing and problem-solving is the way forward. This is particularly important where there is a risk a child will make a false allegation.

I'll say, here and now, that absolutely a child may be telling the truth and that shouldn't be discounted; however, it's not uncommon for adults around traumatised children to come under the spotlight as a result of a false allegation.

Don't sweat the small stuff

Don't empty your magazine of bullets before the real baddies come on the scene. And look out for that shot of adrenaline you get as a result of raising an issue with someone. Is your traumatised body in need of a blast of something? Is Captain Fixy in the house? When we live on our nerves it can feel kind of dull when nothing has happened for a bit, especially when other parts of life have peeled away (friends, hobbies, work). If you recognise yourself here then don't heap the blame on yourself; find some adrenaline elsewhere or do something calming like make yourself a nice herbal tea.[2]

---

2 Then pour it down the sink and fix yourself something really nice.

CHAPTER 16

Supporting Families

Professionals

Whether you are a social worker, youth worker, teacher, teaching assistant, psychologist, therapist, police officer or youth offending officer or in any other professional role that means you work with or come into contact with families raising care-experienced, traumatised children and young people, let me tell you we need you. Knowledgeable and compassionate professionals can make an enormous difference to our ability to cope and to our family's outcomes.

It takes a strong team to raise a child. A strong team is more than a number of people who cheer us along and keep us afloat, although it is partly about this.

I've been around the office block, into consultation rooms, meeting rooms, into County Hall, classrooms, police stations and government buildings enough to know good support and poor support when I see it. This is mostly, but not exclusively, as a result of experiencing good support. I feel bound to point out though that poor support is much worse than a bad day at the office. Poor support is damaging. And in my experience poor support is more often about organisation and systems than it is about individuals.

It has to be said that at the time of writing, resources around children and families have been cut to the bone and I'm not going to make any excuses for that. Good support, however, is about striving to get it right first time; it's preventative, efficient and it evolves with the situation. It also makes jobs more meaningful and satisfying and improves working relationships: a win–win.

This is what I believe good support looks like.

Trauma-informed

Knowing what early adverse experience, that is, trauma, does to a child, how it impacts on their brain development, their relationships and how they experience the world is the key that opens the door to understanding a significant group of children. These are the children who disrupt our classrooms, get excluded from school, who under-perform in exams, who populate waiting lists, who get arrested, who come to the attention of exploitative adults and who develop addictive habits. Economically speaking, these are the children who exert huge life-long demands on the public purse, if they do not get the help and understanding they need, when they need it. They are not the wilfully misbehaving under-class, they are traumatised and their trauma prevents them from pulling themselves out of situations and responding to what we think should help them. Punishing them for what are really trauma-fuelled behaviours, blaming their parents, carers or other adults trying their best, excluding them or striking them from waiting lists can set in motion a set of circumstances that do not end well. I'm not proposing that we allow trauma to run around the streets smashing windows, not at all, I'm just suggesting that if we understand why the running around and why the broken windows, we may arrive at an intervention that works for the long term.

A solid understanding of trauma puts us all in a much better informed position to help this group of children. It gives us all a shared language and it helps us all to problem-solve and support each other. Working with and parenting this group of children is extremely tough.

Listening

Actively listening to therapeutic parents is another fundamental pillar of good support. When a parent shares their deepest and darkest experiences and concerns they need someone to listen and take them seriously. Being pacified may make matters a whole lot worse, even though the pacification may be delivered with the best of intentions. 'Well, all teenagers can be argumentative' may not wash if a parent is trying to explain that his son will not do anything he is asked, including coming in at night, going to bed, going to school and screams in his face and throws furniture when he is asked. Parents, in my experience, do not ask for help with run-of-the-mill parenting. Most are living with way, way, way out there stuff.

Part of active listening, with a trauma-informed ear, is not to fall into the trap of offering inappropriate advice such as 'Have you tried encouraging her to punch a cushion?' or 'Have you considered taking him fishing?' Again, it may be meant with the best of intentions, but risks coming across as insulting and patronising. Most therapeutic parents in my experience are sensible and intelligent folk and if there was an easy answer, they would have found it themselves.

Good listening is very powerful. Do not under-estimate it. So too are the sorts of responses that accept and acknowledge the difficulty such as 'I know this is way above what most parents are living with and I know it's incredibly difficult.'

Honesty

What most families in distress are looking for is an answer to all their struggles, something that will make all the difficulties go away, the right kind of therapy, the right school. As things stand, options are very limited. I would far rather be told that what I'm looking for isn't available, or that someone working with me isn't going to be able to respond quickly because they have two other crises to deal with, than to be strung along. I think when we can all be constructively honest, we can come up with solutions together.

This charming man

It is no secret that children who have had to use whatever skills they can in order to keep themselves safe may count charm amongst these skills. Charm is like rubbing everyone's tummies, it makes us all feel good and praise each other about what progress we are making. It also serves to take our eyes off the ball. If you've never experienced the power of charm, be aware of it and if a parent is warning you that things might not be all that they seem, please take heed. The same also goes for fantasy. If something sounds too good to be true, it just might be. It's easy to get fooled by trauma.

Practical help

Support systems around children and families are pretty good at offering advice and organising a meeting but what they are less skilled at is coming up with practical help: the doing. Discussing something is kind of safe and we can sit in meeting rooms writing notes and agreeing with each other. The doing is sharp end, uncomfortable and challenging and it gets alongside us and helps us out when the s**t has hit the fan. This is what many families need more of, the brave, unsweetened variety of help that can roll its sleeves up and get in amongst our teenagers.

Confidence and knowledge

A confident and knowledgeable professional who can look you in the eye and say, 'I know what to do and I'm going to get on and do it' is a godsend. These professionals are regulating and containing and can allow parents to do what they do best: parent.

It IS personal

All committed, meaningful, long-term permanence options for children require bucket-loads of love, nurture and bonding and this is both the strength and the weakness of solid permanence. When parents become emotional, or act in ways you wish were more sanitized, just bear in mind that for them, this whole situation is personal, not professional. This is their dear loved one who is in this situation and although not their child by birth, this is the child they have walked over hot coals for and who is stitched into them.

We are not who we used to be

Living with a traumatised child changes who you are. Once sensible, eloquent, easy-going people get messed up, not forever, but you may well only come across them at their absolute lowest. Please bear this in mind and treat them with respect and care, scoop them up, show them compassion and do your best for them. And be mindful that they may not be in a strong enough state to accept a heap of advice that requires thought and energy.

Keep in touch

This is basic practice, so I apologise if I am preaching to the choir, but a parent holding a child through a difficult time will be holding out for your call, possibly jumping every time the phone rings and not sleeping well until they have heard from you. Keep in touch, even if all you can manage is a quick email that says, 'I haven't forgotten about you, I hope you're OK and I'll call you tomorrow morning.'

Look after yourselves

It's not only individuals that work with traumatised children and young people that can catch their trauma, it can happen to organisations too. They become demanding and argumentative, they focus on small picky things and ignore the bigger picture, they make awful decisions, treat their staff poorly and they become chaotic and disorganised. They also tend towards a systems response to a human problem. How many therapeutic parents in need of support find themselves on the receiving end of investigations? Loads and loads.

Please, please give yourselves time and space to decompress, to reflect, learn and to come up with creative solutions. Support each other and you will be far more likely to offer good support to those you are tasked with supporting.

A bit about accounting and organisation

A service can either design itself around the customer or client or it can design itself around its own needs. Bureaucratically speaking it's easier to slice up a child's life into, say, age groups or position in the care system, or legal order, and create neat departments and cost centres. As the parent of a child for whom the service exists, it's glaringly obvious to me that the bureaucratic model does not work for those which it seeks to serve. If we are serious about teaching children about permanence and longevity of relationships then we must put a system around them that reinforces these important lessons. We must keep the same professionals alongside them as far as we can, to get to know them, develop robust relationships that last the test of time. And if we are serious about improving the life chances of our most vulnerable children then we should be following their lives, not forcing their lives to fit with the short-termism of the bureaucracy.

Spend-to-save is not rocket science but it will never happen with meaning until we turn our systems and our accounting on their heads. Our young people were denied therapies and interventions that cost several hundred pounds in their early years, and some of those young people are costing the state thousands and thousands of pounds now. That's not to say that early interventions could have made a difference because there are no guarantees but if their therapeutic families break apart and they have to be accommodated (and parented) elsewhere, if they become unemployed, develop addictions or find their way into the criminal justice system, they become mind-blowingly expensive. I wish I could have had a fraction of that money to spend on therapy and, frankly, respite. The cost of one week of residential care, or one spell in the police station custody suite would have made a real difference. That sort of money, at the back end of a young person's journey, when the opportunities for change are running dry is spent like water.

Goodbyes are important
Given that structural difficulties and high staff turnover are the reality for now, I would make a plea for the good goodbye. A good goodbye is better than no goodbye. Our children benefit from learning that adults sometimes change jobs and move on but that they care enough to see them and explain why they are going and to tell them they will be thinking of them.

—

Professionals of all types, we need you, we need you standing alongside us and around our children. We need you to scoop us up when we are on our knees, send us useful resources, call us when we are losing hope, take the reins now and again, get bossy when you need to and celebrate the wins with us. We can't do this without you and with your help we can watch our young people develop and succeed and move into the world with confidence and a bright future ahead of them.

Family and friends

Therapeutic parenting is not possible without the support of family and friends. End of. And yet family and friends don't choose to be the family and friends of those who step forward to become therapeutic parents. You kind of get subsumed into it all and I know that it can be difficult and demanding. I also know that the collateral damage can be significant and all for something you never asked for. I risk getting into some tricky territory but nevertheless here are some ways that you may provide meaningful support to your loved ones.

Be honest

I think it's best to be clear about what kind of support you can and cannot offer. Supporting your loved ones isn't always about the big gestures, it could be something that to you seems minor. Whatever that is, getting these things out in the open, with compassion, can help everyone to know where they stand. I offer a menu of options below from which there may be something that you think you could step in and do. I do hope so because, WE NEED YOU!

Get informed

The greatest help to anyone who is therapeutically parenting usually comes from those who really get what our children are about, what drives them and the type of parenting that they need. Therapeutic parenting is different from more traditional types of parenting and can look sort of flaky and unboundaried. It isn't. It can appear from looking from the outside in, as though what these unruly kids need is a firm set of rules and consequences, a no excuses, no second or third chances approach. Trust me when I tell you that if this worked, we wouldn't even be having this conversation, I wouldn't have written close to 240,000 words on the subject and these kids would be doing what they are told. It's a huge mental adjustment and one that all of us struggle to come to terms with.

If you are reading this chapter on its own, away from the context of the whole book and all the other good books, then your first step is to read the whole thing. Take care because I swear a bit and I'm not in the business of sugaring the pill. If you don't like my style then there are lots of other books on offer and your friend or relative will be able to recommend something suitable.

If you really get into this then try some day courses or conferences. Some of them are really very good.

Soft support

Making a cake, or a shepherd's pie, pushing the vacuum cleaner around, doing some shopping, taking your loved one out for a coffee (literally taking them, including the lifts) are all ways of providing soft but nevertheless useful support. Don't think you have to do the heavy lifting in order to be supportive.

Get to know the children

Our children need a network of kind and trusted adults around them. You don't have to be therapeutically minded in order to be a part of this network, you just need to understand that their past trauma informs the way they operate. Being accepting and playful with them, taking an interest and spending time with them is valuable. And you don't have to do this for hours and hours. Often regular and short is best for them and for you because, let's face it, our kids can be hard work to be around. We don't want you getting ruined as well.

Babysit

Our children will find it difficult to spend time with someone else, when their main parent or carer is out. They will think that their parent or carer has abandoned them. It may take a lot of practice runs before babysitting can be a workable option.

When we think of babysitting we usually think about young children and of course this book is about the teen years. The gap between our child's biological age and developmental age will mean that perhaps they won't cope with being left on their own. For this reason, babysitting will be required beyond what you might expect.

Having someone around who can be with our child allowing us to get out is an absolute gift. If you can offer this, then please, yes.

Overnight stay

If you really are committed to this support business then offering an overnight stay and putting in place the strategies that will help this to be a success will be a great help. Over time, a child will develop a familiarity and it will all get easier. It may be necessary to build in escape plans if for some reason things are not working out.

Advocacy

When things are getting really sticky, your friend or loved one may need some support at a meeting. If they ask you to do this then please consider accepting. They may have asked you because you have certain skills or because you can offer moral support. Read the chapter 'Being an Effective Advocate' for some ideas about how to ace this.

Emergency help

From time to time many therapeutic parents face a crisis of one kind or another. It's incredibly useful to have someone to call on during these times, to either collect a child from school or liaise with someone or whatever. Having that someone who can be flexible and competent, in a no-fuss way is priceless.

An understanding ear

Your friend or relative will benefit greatly from having someone who understands and who can listen without judgement to all their trials and tribulations. It can be a lot to take on board and you may have to hear things that are not within your usual realm of normal but being there with love, strength and compassion is a real help.

—

Whatever it is that you can offer to your friend or relative will be making the world a better place. You will be helping that special someone in your life to continue doing a great job for a child who needs and deserves the best. Thank you.

CHAPTER 17

Onward

When we take our first steps into becoming therapeutic parents, we take a leap of faith and as our children grow up we take on the challenges and celebrate the successes with them. Sometimes things don't turn out quite how we had planned or hoped for and family life can at times be excruciatingly difficult. We learn along the way and adjust and gather our supporters around us and we put one foot in front of the other, travel through the dark forest and the sunlit fields and we reach the point at which the journey isn't ours to take any longer. Our children grow into young adults and take the reins and we have to step back and let them make their own way, helping out where we can and when they allow us to.

Our job as therapeutic parents is to ensure our eventual redundancy and yet our children are our life's work. We develop ways of seeing into their world and we build structure around them to help bridge them into independence. So much of our work is about scaffolding, building and rebuilding and through doing this we learn about the highs and lows of humanity, its ability for hurt and destruction and its ability for repair and incredible resilience and love. We are changed forever in ways that regular parents are perhaps not. Many of us might say we are better people as a result of parenting our children. Acceptance, sacrifice, empathy, optimism, dogged determination: it's a parenting bootcamp that surely sends us up a few rungs on the ladder of enlightenment.

Therapeutic parenting is by its very nature an imperfect art. We do our best and so do our children and at the end of it we are all still a work-in-progress and we come to realise that we are going to have to stand in the wings for a long time to come, cheering on and dishing out nurture while the faltering steps into adulthood are taken.

Our best has to be good enough and is good enough. And what is left when the majority of the hard parenting work is done is you. You have done and continue to do something incredible for your child. You have held on when others might not have, you have laughed and cried with them, picked them up, shaken off the shame and let the pride shine through. The expertise and sheer sticking power and love that I experience in a room of therapeutic parents really is like nothing else. It is awesome. You are awesome.

What you must do though is keep something of you back because you are precious. You will need that something when your child takes the reins for themselves. This part, when they grab the reins, may not be pretty and your success and ability to come through will depend on how much of you is left intact. Value and nurture yourself because you really are worth it. Play, laugh, explore, rediscover yourself and find new beginnings because it's not just the end of something, it's the beginning of something too.

I end here with two thank yous.

Thank you for reading my work. I don't know how I would have kept afloat over these years of therapeutic parenting without having writing as a creative and campaigning outlet. You have done me a great favour.

And thank you for doing what you do for the children who don't just get over it. You are doing something amazing. Don't forget that.

No Matter What
An Adoptive Family's Story of Hope, Love and Healing
Sally Donovan

Paperback: £9.99 / $16.95
ISBN: 978 1 84905 431 7
eISBN: 978 0 85700 781 0

352 pages

'I love you, no matter what.'

An uplifting true story of an ordinary couple who build an extraordinary family, No Matter What describes how Sally and Rob Donovan embark upon a journey to adopt following a diagnosis of infertility.

Sally Donovan brings to life with characteristic wit and honesty the difficulties of living with infertility, their decision to adopt and the bewildering process involved. Finally matched with young siblings Jaymey and Harlee, Sally and Rob's joy turns to shock as they discover disturbing details of their children's past and realise that they must do everything it takes to heal their children.

By turns tragic, inspiring and hilarious, Sally and Rob's story offers a rare insight into the world of adoptive parents and just what it takes to bring love to the lives of traumatised children.

The Unofficial Guide to Adoptive Parenting
The Small Stuff, The Big Stuff and The Stuff In Between
Sally Donovan

Paperback: £12.99 / $19.95
ISBN: 978 1 84905 536 9
eISBN: 978 0 85700 959 3

232 pages

This is not just another book about adoptive parenting. This is the real stuff: dynamic, messy, baffling adoptive parenting, rooted in domestic life.

Award-winning columnist and adoptive parent Sally Donovan offers savvy, compassionate advice on how to be 'good enough' in the face of both day-to-day and more bewildering challenges – how to respond to 'red mist' meltdowns, crippling anxieties about new routines and, most importantly, how to meet the intimidating challenge of being strong enough to protect and nurture your child.

Full of affecting and hilarious stories drawn from life in the Donovan household, *The Unofficial Guide to Adoptive Parenting* offers parents a refreshing counterblast to stuffy parenting manuals -- read it, weep, laugh and learn.

Billy Bramble and The Great Big Cook Off
A Story about Overcoming Big, Angry Feelings at Home and at School
Sally Donovan
Illustrated by Kara McHale

Paperback: £8.99 / $13.95
ISBN: 978 1 84905 663 2
eISBN: 978 1 78450 164 8

192 pages

"Want to know something else about me? I am Billy Bramble: the King, the President and the Emperor of Bad Lucksville. I am the Chief Executive of Bad Luck Limited, the Bad Luck Champion of the World, the Bad Luck Guinness World Record holder and it's all thanks to my invisible dog Gobber. He's my Bringer of Bad Luck."

Billy Bramble likes rude words, smelly farts, loud farts and freestyle sneezing but when BAD THINGS happen, his invisible angry dog Gobber barks in his ears, gives him brain mash and breaks things. One day a competition is announced at school – The Great Big Cook Off – can Billy Bramble defeat Gobber and change his epic bad luck?

An irreverent story for children aged 8–12 about a less than perfect boy, this book will inspire any child who's ever secretly thought they might be less than perfect too.

The A-Z of Therapeutic Parenting
Strategies and Solutions
Sarah Naish

Paperback: £15.99 / $22.95
ISBN: 978 1 78592 376 0
eISBN: 978 1 78450 732 9

344 pages

Therapeutic parenting is a deeply nurturing parenting style, and is especially effective for children with attachment difficulties, or who experienced childhood trauma. This book provides everything you need to know in order to be able to effectively therapeutically parent.

Providing a model of intervention, *The A–Z of Therapeutic Parenting* gives parents or caregivers an easy to follow process to use when responding to issues with their children. The following A–Z covers 60 common problems parents face, from acting aggressively to difficulties with sleep, with advice on what might trigger these issues, and how to respond.

Easy to navigate and written in a straightforward style, this book is a 'must-have' for all therapeutic parents.

Sarah Naish is an adoptive parent, director of Inspire Training Group, which delivers training on attachment issues, founder of the National Association of Therapeutic Parents and author of the hugely popular *Therapeutic Parenting Books* series.

Therapeutic Parenting Essentials
Moving from Trauma to Trust
Sarah Naish, Sarah Dillon and Jane Mitchell

Paperback: £16.99 / $24.95
ISBN: 978 1 78775 031 9
eISBN: 978 1 78775 032 6

336 pages

All families of children affected by trauma are on a journey, and this book will help to guide you and your family on your journey from trauma to trust.

Sarah Naish shares her own experiences of adopting five siblings. She describes how to use therapeutic parenting – a deeply nurturing parenting style – to overcome common challenges when raising children who have experienced trauma. The book describes a series of difficult episodes for her family, exploring both parent's and child's experiences of the same events – with the child's experience written by a former fostered child – and in doing so reveals the very good reasons why traumatized children behave as they do. The book explores the misunderstandings that grow between parents and their children, and provides comfort to the reader – you are not the only family going through this!

Full of insights from a family which has really been there, this book gives you advice and strategies to help you and your family thrive.

Sarah Naish is an adoptive parent, director of Inspire Training Group, founder of the National Association of Therapeutic Parents and author of the hugely popular Therapeutic Parenting Books series.

Sarah Dillon spent much of her childhood in foster care, and is now an attachment therapist and Panel Chair.

Jane Mitchell is an adoptive parent, and specialises in training around attachment, developmental trauma and related neuroscience.